Students and External Readers	Staff & Research Students
DATE DUE FOR RETURN	**DATE OF ISSUE**

14 MAR 84

14. MAR 84

27. JUN 84

19. 03. 90

02. MAR 92

18. MAR 91   UNIVERSITY LIBRARY

18. MAR 91   SEM

0 4 JUN 2003

27. JUN 91

N.B. All books must be returned for the Annual Inspection in June

Wallace Stevens' "Whole Harmonium"

RICHARD ALLEN BLESSING

SYRACUSE UNIVERSITY PRESS

Manufactured in the United States of America

To my mother,
my father,
my wife and my son.

RICHARD ALLEN BLESSING, a native of Bradford, Pennsylvania, received his undergraduate education at Hamilton College and his M.A. and Ph.D. degrees from Tulane University. He is assistant professor of English, specializing in American literature, at Heidelberg College, Tiffin, Ohio. He has also taught at Louisiana State University in New Orleans.

6 000 668417

Contents

Preface

The Collected Poems of Wallace Stevens, first published in
1954, is seen here as a single, unified, grand poem, "The
Whole of Harmonium," as Stevens himself once preferred
to call it. My attempt to illustrate the unity of *The Collected
Poems* has led to some methodological ironies. For instance,
a glance at my contents page will reveal that my plan of
organization seems to divide rather than unify. Each of my
chapters corresponds to a division in *The Collected Poems,*
and each of those divisions, of course, corresponds to a
previously published volume of poetry by Wallace Stevens.
Moreover, the reader will soon discover that my critical approach is usually that of explication, and that consequently
I spend most of my pages working with individual poems,
with "pieces" rather than with "The Whole of Harmonium."
I find myself dissecting an organic whole in order to demonstrate that it is, in fact, an organic whole.

There are, however, some points which might be offered
in behalf of my approach. First, transitions between chapters here are intended to indicate the manner in which one
volume of the poetry of Wallace Stevens grows naturally
into another. Second, in explicating individual poems, I
have concentrated heavily on those poems that change most
significantly in meaning or value as a result of being placed

in the context of "The Whole of Harmonium." In all cases, the explications are intended to illustrate the way in which the individual poem is a stage in a larger dynamic process. Third, this study to some extent emulates the movement that takes place in "The Whole of Harmonium." That is, as I move from chapter to chapter I become increasingly less concerned with individual and particular lines, images, and ideas and increasingly more concerned with the poetic theory that unifies Stevens' grand poem, *The Collected Poems of Wallace Stevens*. Finally, I hope that in the final pages of the book, particularly in the "Afterword," I have put back together any pieces that I might have scattered about earlier.

In any study of this length, one incurs debts of gratitude to be acknowledged. I am especially grateful to Professors E. Phillip Bollier and Richard P. Adams of Tulane University for their criticisms and encouragement. Professor Bollier was kind enough to read the many rough drafts of my study, and his suggestions were invariably (and sometimes maddeningly) correct. I owe my original interest in Stevens to Professor Adams, but I owe him a much greater debt for his friendship, faith, and wise counsel. It would be unfair to place upon that gentleman the burden of responsibility for my prose style, but without his strenuous efforts, gentle reader, things would be much worse.

Professor K. Raeburn Miller of the Louisiana State University in New Orleans also deserves special mention here. A cherished friend and my favorite poet, Professor Miller has taught me many things, some of them about poetry and Wallace Stevens.

The dedication of a book to my mother and father is an appropriate, though scarcely adequate, payment for the sacrifices that they made to educate their son. My gratitude to them for my education, and for so much more than my education, is but feebly suggested by my dedication.

If it were not for my wife, I should take no pleasure in

this publication. Every man writes, in some sense, for one ideal reader. And I write for her. My two-year-old son, in all candor, has been little help in the preparation of this manuscript. At times, in fact, he has been downright detrimental to its progress. But he remains my most uncritical admirer, and one cannot disregard that. I hope that he may one day take pleasure in the fact that his father once dedicated a book to him.

I am grateful to Alfred A. Knopf for permission to quote from the following copyrighted editions: *The Collected Poems of Wallace Stevens* (1954), *Opus Posthumous* (1957), *The Necessary Angel* (1951), and *The Letters of Wallace Stevens* (1966). In my manuscript I have noted references to the letters of Stevens, but I have given page references to the other three books parenthetically. I have used "CP" to stand for *The Collected Poems*, "OP" to stand for *Opus Posthumous*, and "NA" to stand for *The Necessary Angel*. Full bibliographical information can be found in the "Selected Bibliography" at the end of this volume.

Wallace Stevens'
"Whole Harmonium"

Introduction

The scholar who begins a lengthy study of Wallace Stevens
at this time senses the need to answer two questions. The
first, likely to be posed by undergraduate students and non-
specialists, is simply, "Why a book on Wallace Stevens?" It
is not an unreasonable question. After all, unlike Eliot,
Pound, Cummings, Edna St. Vincent Millay, and Dorothy
Canfield Fisher, Wallace Stevens is not among those literary figures listed in *Webster's New World Dictionary*. He is
not popularly or widely known, even by name, and he is certainly not widely read. And it is unlikely that he ever will be.

Yet perhaps it is time to be dogmatic about it. Wallace
Stevens is a poet worth knowing; indeed, he is one of the
great poets of our century and is among the greatest of all
the American poets. And he is such for the simplest and
best of reasons. He wrote a great poet's share of great
poetry and much more poetry that is merely very, very
good, and, to the delight of the Stevens specialist, Stevens,
even when performing poetic finger exercises, is intensely
interesting. The past twenty years have seen bestowed upon
him those tangible emblems of poetic success that give
aid and comfort to the reader who senses in the solitude
of his study that Stevens is one of our handful of master
poets. He has won a number of prizes—a Bollingen Prize,
BOLLOCKS

BULLSHITTER

two National Book Awards, and a Pulitzer Prize; he has
increasingly received the highest praise from other poets
and from our most respected critics; and, especially in the
past ten years, he has been the subject of intense and
generally laudatory critical scrutiny. In fact, I doubt that
any other poet of our century has managed to withstand so
many recent dissertations, *Explicator* explications, assorted
journal articles, and book-length studies. For example,
since 1958 there have been no fewer than ten books published on Stevens, not to mention three book-length collec-
tions of critical essays, a concordance, and an edition of
The Letters of Wallace Stevens.

It is the breadth and bulk of Stevens scholarship in the
past decade that raises the second question to be answered
by one at the start of a long work on Stevens. The specialist
and professional scholar may ask, quite appropriately,
"Why *another* book on Stevens?" In short, in what way is
this book distinct from the others already in the field? The
answer, I believe, is that mine is the first study of Stevens to
treat *The Collected Poems of Wallace Stevens* as a single,
organic, and highly dynamic grand poem. And that is a very
important distinction.

In his 1951 *PMLA* article, "Toward a Theory of Romanticism," Morse Peckham declared that "The artist is the man
who creates a symbol of the truth. He can think metaphori-
cally, and, if the world is an organic structure, only a
statement with the organic complexity of the work of art
can create an adequate symbol of it." Stevens, an artist
trying to create an adequate symbol for the truth in the
twentieth century, found the world to be so without structure, so dynamic, so much in process, that the fixed form of
any individual poem could not adequately represent those
flowing interchanges of imagination and phenomenal universe which constitute the way of things for modern man.
Thus, in order to do critical justice to the poetry of Wallace
Stevens, we must read him with the awareness that the

individual poems are not his great achievement, that *The Collected Poems of Wallace Stevens* is his unified "grand poem," for only that large and complex work is capable of adequately representing his view of the flow of experience in a world in process.

There is some external evidence which suggests that Stevens hoped from the time of his first published volume to create just such a unified poetic symbol for the world. In 1923 Stevens wrote Alfred Knopf to suggest that a suitable title for the volume which ultimately was published as *Harmonium* might be *The Grand Poem: Preliminary Minutiae*.[1] Although a week later Stevens changed his mind and wired Knopf tersely, "Use Harmonium,"[2] the idea of the "grand poem" to which the earlier works were but "preliminaries" seems never to have left him. In 1954, looking back over more than a third of a century of writing poetry, Stevens again wrote Knopf, this time concerning the search for a suitable title for the book which the poet, dreading the implied finality of a "collection," had put off as long as Knopf would let him. "I thought of all the objections which you suggest in your letter of May 24 to the title THE WHOLE OF HARMONIUM and brushed them aside. But with all those wise people you speak of thinking that the thing should be called THE COLLECTED POEMS OF WALLACE STEVENS, a machine-made title if there ever was one, it is all right with me."[3] The testiness of Stevens' acquiescence is that of an artist who recognized the inappropriateness of a "machine-made" title to an organic work of art. The term "collection" suggests a bringing together of disparate parts without implying that the parts are intended to form a whole. Stevens realized, as his publisher apparently did not, that the poems of *The Rock* grow out of the poems of *Harmonium* as naturally and organically as the

---

[1] Stevens, *Letters*, p. 237.
[2] Ibid., p. 238.
[3] Ibid., p. 834.

leaves of a tree emerge from its stem. Despite its title, Knopf's publication of *The Collected Poems of Wallace Stevens* is the publication of "The Whole of Harmonium," for the poetry of Wallace Stevens is an ongoing process, a dynamic symbol for the process of life itself.

Other Stevens critics have been aware of the close relationships that exist among the poems of Wallace Stevens, though none has, to my knowledge, seen *The Collected Poems* as a single complex symbol. In the first book-length study of Stevens' work, William Van O'Connor pointed to the fact that

> The abstractness of the later poetry is in part in the mind of the reader who fails to perceive the complexity and to feel the weight of meaning borne by the symbols and characters that live in his mythology. A full examination of this mythology would require a very extensive study of individual images, symbols and figures recurring and growing by accretion from poem to poem over more than forty years.[4]

More recent critical works also focus on Stevens' "growth," though the emphasis is sometimes different from O'Connor's. Joseph Riddel, for example, believes that "Stevens' changes in style and idea were progressive and cumulative, that his poetic development was synonymous with a growth in self-awareness."[5] I agree with both O'Connor and Riddel, for it is certainly true that Stevens' work does embody the kind of growth each man mentions. However, it might be said that most poets change in style and idea as they mature and find their subjects, and certainly many poets develop by long association a kind of private world of symbols and images.

What makes Stevens unique is that his changes in technique, subject matter, imagery, and tone all grow naturally

[4] O'Connor, *The Shaping Spirit*, p. 31.
[5] Taken from the dust jacket of Riddel's *Clairvoyant Eye.*

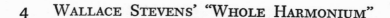

out of a dynamic and organic view of experience, life, and poetry. His changes in style and technique, his shifts in subject matter, his tonal variations, and his evolving image patterns are all essential to his presentation of an adequate symbol of the world in which whirl and motion are the uncomfortable but irreducible facts by which we live.

"Things seen," Stevens once said, "are things as seen" (OP, p. 162). *The Collected Poems*, seen as a single complex symbol rather than as a gallery of individual pieces, becomes a new poem, a poem that acquires new significance and requires new examination on the part of Stevens critics. The individual poems within the grand poem immediately are placed in a context, and, as Stevens knew, a change in context is a change in significance and, frequently, a change in meaning and value.

There are, of course, other changes. The movement from the concrete, sensory, sun-drenched poetry of *Harmonium* to the abstract, meditative, autumnal poetry of *The Rock* becomes more than a development of poetic craftsmanship; it becomes the mirror of all human experience. The modern poet who tries to create a symbol for human experience must take into consideration the fact that immediate sensory contact with the world of external objects is but the beginning of "experience." The mind must order and make coherent the evidence of the senses; the imagination must work its inevitable and myriad transformations; reason must place this sensory evidence in its proper relationship to other such evidence; and meditation upon the process by which the sensory data becomes part of what we know must place the data (and us) in some relationship to the world in which we live. In short, Stevens knew that experience is a process, and that the instant of sensory stimulation is only the barest beginning of that process. And he knew also that only the grand poem, the adequate symbol for organic life, could present the process in a fashion true to the facts of the dynamic relationship between man and his world.

Stevens becomes a poet of even greater stature when one views *The Collected Poems* as "The Whole of Harmonium" rather than as an assortment of individual poems. Most immediately, such an approach shows Stevens to be too serious an artist, too good a poet, to content himself with writing poetry *about* a dynamic world. Such poetry would be philosophy in verse, and poetry should *present* life, not merely make statements about it. Thus, in the continually shifting techniques, subjects, images, moods, and tones of *The Collected Poems* Wallace Stevens demonstrates his solution to the modern poet's problem of how to present growth, motion, and organicism in a work of art.

Moreover, such a view of Stevens' "Whole Harmonium" reveals him to be an artist capable of designing and creating a poem on the grand scale, a work of monumental breadth and scope. As a unified attempt to symbolize the growth and development experienced by a creative human being, "The Whole of Harmonium" is a poem which may stand comparison with the major poems of the English language. In subject and intention, for example, Stevens' grand poem is quite similar to Wordsworth's *Prelude*. The difference is that Wordsworth's "spots of time" are presented in the past tense as dramatic reflections, while Stevens' are experienced immediately as part of a continuously flowing process. However, my point is simply that Stevens' "grand poem" deserves to be measured against one of the more enormous poetic undertakings in literary history.

Finally, Stevens' "Whole Harmonium" proves him to be among the most modern, if not the most modern, of our twentieth-century poets. Like the physicist, Stevens saw beneath the illusory surface of our world to the whirling vortex of the atom. He knew that life is motion and that structure is illusion. Like most of us moderns he felt from time to time the discomforts of motion sickness, and like most of us he felt a "blessed rage for order" in the face of the uncertainties of whirl and flux. He knew, or came to know, that to give form and beauty to what is essentially without form or beauty is to falsify, that to fix "reality" even momentarily is to create a fiction. But he came to know, too, that the final belief must be in a fiction and that the courageous man knows that it must be so and chooses carefully and well. Stevens' attempt to create a symbol for the dynamic process is an affirmation of modern man's will to believe in an order and to create the beautiful in a universe he knows full well to be chaotic. The attempt to make an artistic symbol for a world in process is, perhaps, quixotic, but Stevens' effort to make comprehensible in poetry our incomprehensible human experience is a brave one, and such bravery can help sustain us as we speed toward the twenty-first century.

Harmonium

The world of *Harmonium* is an unfallen world in which the poet rejoices at the beauty of the physical universe; it is, in many ways, an Edenic world, a place in which the awful separation of man from his setting is sometimes overcome and in which an almost childlike delight is taken in the abundance of the earth. The atmosphere is lovely; *Harmonium* is a sun-drenched place, a world of cocks and blackbirds and ripening strawberries, a place of light and of the green of growing things and of violent color, an orchard of rotting apples all the more beautiful for their rotting, a state of mind in which Stevens accepts joyfully the cosmic turmoil and change and seldom, if ever, allows himself to deny by any thought or wish the tenuous, ever-ebbing beauty of the human condition. As Joseph Riddel puts it, the poetry of *Harmonium* demands "a return to innocence, a beginning over. . . . And where best begin but with the old language (making the world new in words which, used in a new way, are renewed) and with new eyes (personae like Peter Quince, the Emersonian Hoon, or Crispin, the parody of innocence who ends by accepting the world outside Eden)?" [1]

[1] Riddel, *Clairvoyant Eye*, p. 53.

The poetry of *Harmonium* is an external poetry which looks outward for the most part and which is heavy with direct appeal to the senses. The most common appeal is, of course, that to the visual sense, and some of the finest moments in all of Stevens' verse occur in *Harmonium* when he evokes pictures of the lushness of this earth. The concluding lines of "Sunday Morning" will serve as an example of such a moment.

> Deer walk upon our mountains, and the quail
> Whistle about us their spontaneous cries;
> Sweet berries ripen in the wilderness;
> And, in the isolation of the sky,
> At evening, casual flocks of pigeons make
> Ambiguous undulations as they sink,
> Downward to darkness, on extended wings.
>
> (CP, p. 70)

Even more remarkable, perhaps, is Stevens' ability to appeal to the kinesthetic sense, to make a reader feel heat and cold and rapid movement and delight in dance-like grace. The ability to elicit a physical reaction, to make a reader aware of chill, is, I suppose, little more than a tour de force, but note the contrast which is formed to the usual sun-warmed tone of *Harmonium* by these lines from "The Snow Man":

> One must have a mind of winter . . .
>
> And have been cold a long time
> To behold the junipers shagged with ice,
> The spruces rough in the distant glitter
>
> Of the January sun; and not to think
> Of any misery in the sound of the wind,
> In the sound of a few leaves . . .
>
> (CP, p. 10)

The ability to evoke a sense of moment, is, however, more significant in terms of Stevens' ability to create an adequate verbal symbol for the experience of life, for the poet who cannot capture motion in his idiom and rhythm cannot adequately present life. Certainly Stevens' successful evocation of the kinesthetic sense is responsible for whatever pleasure we take in the poem which he entitles simply "Life Is Motion."

> In Oklahoma,
> Bonnie and Josie,
> Dressed in calico,
> Danced around a stump.
> They cried,
> "Ohoyaho,
> Ohoo" . . .
> Celebrating the marriage
> Of flesh and air.
>   (CP, p. 83)

The "intellectual" content of the poem is almost nonexistent. The poem resists criticism precisely because it is purely a poem of joy in its own dance. The short lines, never containing more than three accents and usually containing but two, suggest rapid movement. The spaciousness of Oklahoma is the setting, and the motionless, central stump serves only to emphasize by contrast the movement and the emptiness which surround it. The cry which Bonnie and Josie utter is mindless and without meaning, a cry of pure and innocent celebration of the miraculous union of man and his universe, of the human flesh and the air which makes the climate in which we live. Only the unfallen experience life so, and the diminutive endings of the names "Bonnie" and "Josie," taken together with the actions of the two figures, suggest that they are children.

"Earthy Anecdote," the very first work of *The Collected Poems*, seems to be a similar exercise in the stimulation of the kinesthetic sense. The experience of this poem is straightforward enough: The bucks race across the plains of Oklahoma, swerving from side to side in an attempt to avoid the "firecat," apparently a prairie fire. There are, one is sure, no symbols being employed here. Rather we are caught up in the sensation of sweep and rapid movement across the emptiness of Oklahoma. Life, Stevens insists again, is motion, and the settling of the firecat at the end of the poem implies a permanence and motionlessness which is most ominous. There is more than a hint of satiation in this settling, a suggestion that the bucks have met death in the form of the firecat and that they are swerving and clattering in their swift, circular line no more.

The same qualities—sense of movement and lack of abstract meaning—can be found in other of the poetic experiences of *Harmonium*. "The Load of Sugar-Cane" is an example, and so is "Ploughing on Sunday." "Ploughing on Sunday," like "Life Is Motion," is made up of short lines of two accents which give a sense of rapid and almost violent motion. The verbs, except for "I'm ploughing," are all in the simple present tense. The tail of the white cock "tosses," and that of the turkey-cock "glitters." The wind "pours" down, and the feathers of the cocks "flare," "bluster," "stream," and "spread." The verb forms give a sense of immediacy to these perceptions, while the central experience, that of ploughing, is described as process, as a continuing action. The poet is plough*ing*, for, like nothing else in the landscape of North America which he farms, his activity is conscious, planned, and purposeful. The shining sun and the movement of the cock feathers are, in contrast, happenings which "occur as they occur." The human activity is interwoven with the activity of nature, and the human spirit mingles with the earth itself, as the act of ploughing would indicate. The fact that the ploughing, the human activity, takes place on Sunday indicates, though most subtly, that the jubilant human being who occupies the structural center of the poem and the physical center of the stage-setting of North America is at one with his environment because he is *not* at one with his society and its religious rituals. For such a man, cock and sun and the casual relationships between cock and sun are enough. They are what will suffice.

As the quotation from Riddel which I cited earlier pointed out, *Harmonium* is a book of "new eyes," a volume which employs a variety of dramatic personas including Hoon, Crispin, and Peter Quince. The dramatic mask and the dramatic setting are devices which almost disappear in the later volumes, for dramatization is a way of externalizing experience. That is, any thought or abstract idea may be projected into the world, given a local habitation and a name, and made to act and speak. In *Harmonium,* even problems in metaphysics and philosophy are made concrete and dramatic experiences, whereas in *Transport to Summer* or in *Auroras of Autumn* one finds that Stevens is much more prone to concentrate on the "meaning of the capture" of even the simplest object in the physical universe.

The most pervasive metaphysical problem in *Harmonium* is one that emerges quite naturally from Stevens' concern with the interworkings of the imagination and reality. The basic issue is most conveniently set forth in the two notes from "The Comedian as the Letter C." The poem opens with the aphoristic "Man is the intelligence of his soil, the sovereign ghost," while Section IV, *"The Idea of a Colony,"* begins with "his soil is man's intelligence./ That's better. That's worth crossing seas to find." These lines have been much commented upon. Hi Simons has defined the terms involved by stating that *"intelligence* means spirit and *soil* is the form of synecdoche that consists in naming a part instead of a whole." [2] The question is that of whether man is a function of his environment or the creator of his environment by the shaping power of his imagination.

Joseph Riddel takes Stevens-Crispin at his word in this

[2] Simons, " 'The Comedian as the Letter C,' " p. 98.

matter, affirming that the second nota, "his soil is man's intelligence," is the "true aesthetic ratio." [3] However, I believe that John Enck is nearer the truth in his more cautious evaluation of the two aphorisms. He says of "his soil is man's intelligence" that "Neither taking such truisms at face value, nor equating them with Stevens' whole outlook, one notices that this manner more nearly resembles the method which *Harmonium* regards favorably." [4]

The most obvious dramatic projections of the notion that man's spirit is shaped by his environment are the respective speakers of "Bantams in Pine-Woods" and "Anecdote of Men by the Thousand." Later on, in *Parts of a World,* the rabbit hero of "A Rabbit as King of the Ghosts" suggests the same idea negatively by his humorously foolish insistence that man (or rabbit) is the intelligence of his soil.

"Bantams in Pine-Woods" dramatizes the conflict between the subjective and the objective world views in the personas of the Chieftan of Azcan and the inchling of the pines. In one of the best critiques of this poem, Marius Bewley observes that "Two extreme interpretations which would contradict each other seem possible, depending on whom one chooses as the villain of the piece, Azcan or the inchling." [5] Bewley decides that Azcan is the "preferable hero," but at the same time acknowledges the attractiveness of the evidence which William Van O'Connor has offered in favor of the inchling as hero.

The reason for the apparent disagreement between Bewley and O'Connor is perhaps to be found in the fact that Stevens is very much uncommitted in the final analysis as to what the true relationship of the artist to his environment is or, indeed, as to what it ought to be. In "Bantams in Pine-Woods," as in his other dramatic monologues, Stevens is experimenting, adopting a temporary posture from which

[3] Riddel, *Clairvoyant Eye,* p. 98.
[4] Enck, *Wallace Stevens,* p. 88.
[5] Bewley, "The Poetry of Wallace Stevens," p. 143.

to study the relationship which is his concern. If this is so, the hero of "Bantams in Pine-Woods" is the inchling-narrator, for we have no internal evidence to the contrary which would favor Azcan. Azcan will have his chance, but when we hear from him he is a tea guest at the Palaz of Hoon and the inchling is gone from the stage.

The dramatic tension in "Bantams in Pine-Woods" is between externalized metaphysical positions, the "Your world is you," which the inchling attributes to Azcan, and the inchling's own affirmation that "I am my world." Azcan's vanity is suggested by the pomp and splendor of his physical appearance, and the accusation that he sees the sun as no more than "blackamoor to bear [his] blazing tail" suggests the foolishness of the man who believes that the universe is created for and by mankind, that "the light is rabbit-light" as the King of the Ghosts is to put it. Azcan believes himself to be the intelligence of his soil. The inchling sees himself and his poetry as being products of his world, a poetry shaped from the bristling pines which surround him. The question of the artist's relationship to his environment finds an answer in the inchling's irascible assertions, but the answer is not to be taken as Stevens' own.

In "Anecdote of Men by the Thousand," a poem which could easily have been turned into a meditation, Stevens again employs a speaker to avoid final responsibility for the metaphysical proposition which opens the poem. The title suggests that many men, men by the thousands, fulfill the opening thesis. "The soul, he said, is composed/ Of the external world" (CP, p. 51). Perhaps both the title and the qualified form, "There are men," which is used instead of "All men," are meant to indicate a limitation which Stevens felt about the metaphysical position taken in the poem.

There are men whose words
Are as natural sounds
Of their places

As the cackle of toucans
In the place of toucans.

The mandoline is the instrument
Of a place.
                    (CP, pp. 51–52)

The inchling of the pines finds that the pines become a part
of his poetry, and that his dress, the fiction in which he
cloaks himself, "Is an invisible element of that place/ Made
visible" (CP, p. 52).

On the other hand, the great spokesman for the self as
intelligence of its soil is the speaker of the well-known "Tea
at the Palaz of Hoon." Most critics assume the speaker to be
Hoon himself, though why Hoon should "descend" to his
own palaz is difficult to ascertain. It seems more likely that
Hoon is the host, and that the speaker is a tea guest who is
somewhat bewildered by the magical influences which
make up the atmosphere of the palaz.

What was the ointment sprinkled on my beard?
What were the hymns that buzzed beside my ears?
What was the sea whose tide swept through me there?
                    (CP, p. 65)

Joseph Riddel is one who takes Hoon himself to be the
narrator, and he sees Hoon as representing "the self in all
its potential, the imagination . . . at the height of its
powers, eloquent and commanding." [6] Bewley agrees that
the voice of "Tea at the Palaz of Hoon" speaks for imagination at its most powerful, arguing that the narrator "had
recreated the external world in his imagination, and in
doing so had elevated it onto a plane in which the world of
fixed objects escaped its static and excluding definition in
space." [7] In Bewley's view, Stevens himself has been a guest
at Hoon's palaz.

However, it seems that Stevens is neither Hoon nor Cris-

[6] Riddel, *Clairvoyant Eye*, p. 65.
[7] Bewley, "The Poetry of Wallace Stevens," p. 149.

pin; rather he employs these personas to probe various positions along the metaphysical spectrum between a purely subjective and a purely objective view of the universe. When we consider the range of positions taken by the various dramatic voices which Stevens employs in *Harmonium*, we will be most hesitant to accept any one of those voices as Stevens' own or as his "true" voice.

The poem which seems to be the most successful of the dramatic projections of the question of whether man is the intelligence of his soil or his soil man's intelligence is the much maligned "Metaphors of a Magnifico." Yvor Winters dismisses the poem as "willful nonsense," and John Enck complains that "the cutting into arbitrary segments, the intrusion of futile echoes, the doubts at the end, and the deliberate flatness in links like 'Of what was it I was thinking?' demonstrate the dangers which vers libre faces." Most or all of these dangers can be explained away, and when Enck goes on to say that "Because a Magnifico need not deign to limit his metaphors, the permutations might roll onward: why not one man on one bridge into twenty villages, every journey being an identical quiescence for the travellers until its end when they resume their separate routes?" [8] he indicates a failure to place the Magnifico's words in their proper relationship to the metaphysical theme which concerns Stevens throughout *Harmonium*.

A Magnifico is a superior being, perhaps because he lives by neither of Crispin's notes, but is aware of both and ponders both without the limited viewpoint of either Hoon or inchling. The divisions, far from being arbitrary, represent obvious dramatic movements in the Magnifico's mind. Unlike Stevens' other monologists, the Magnifico speaks in the present tense; the action of the poem is still going on.

The opening situation is dramatic. Apparently the Magnifico is journeying with the booted men, for the scene shifts

[8] Enck, *Wallace Stevens*, p. 17.

from the bridge to the white walls of the village as if the speaker were in motion, his perspective constantly changing. The opening aphorism,

> Twenty men crossing a bridge,
> Into a village,
> Are twenty men crossing twenty bridges,
> Into twenty villages,
>   (CP, p. 19)

might well have been written by Hoon's tea guest. It suggests intense individuality, that man is indeed the creator of what he sees. Twenty men will see twenty villages because as the intelligence of his soil each man will transform the village into something different from what each other man may see.

It is impossible to determine whether the "Or" which introduces the next metaphysical proposition is meant to be an "exclusive or" or an "inclusive" one. I suspect that Stevens himself is not sure whether or not both propositions can be true at the same time. At any rate, the dictum that twenty men crossing a bridge into a village may equally well be "one man/ Crossing a single bridge into a village" is the absolute statement of the notion that man's soil is his intelligence. Given the same soil, the same bridge and village, all men are the same—are, in effect, one man.

The Magnifico dismisses the problem with the weary admission that the question of the relationship between subject and object, artist and environment, is "old song/ That will not declare itself." The next segment is a simple abstract statement of things as they are.

> Twenty men crossing a bridge,
> Into a village,
> Are
> Twenty men crossing a bridge
> Into a village.
>   (CP, p. 19)

The new position of the "Are" in a line by itself balanced between equal halves of the proposition emphasizes the equality of the statement.

The next segment, however, is more concrete. We no longer deal with the men as abstract entities in a metaphysical problem, but as actual figures in a physical universe. The final lines of the segment, "Of what was it I was thinking?/ So the meaning escapes," suggest that "meaning" is lost in the certainty of physical experience. The only things which finally declare themselves are "The first white wall of the village \ . . ./ The fruit trees . . ." (CP, p. 19). The Magnifico has ceased speculation and turns to physical phenomena, to the external world. As is entirely appropriate to the tenor of *Harmonium,* the Magnifico chooses perception over conception. What is gained? As Rilke puts it in his ninth elegy,

> Just to say: house
> bridge, well, gate, jug, fruit, tree, window—
> at most: column, tower—but to say it, understand,
> oh, to say it as the things themselves never thought
> of existing intensely.

There is no way of unraveling the metaphysical problem posed by the first stanza of "Metaphors of a Magnifico." The isolation of the human condition will not permit; try as we will, we cannot know whether twenty men become one. We are forced to make a statement of fact, certain as meaning, yet valueless, abstract, and admitting of failure. And we, as impoverished failures, turn to poetry, to the expression of the phenomenal universe in heightened and intensified form. The metaphysical polemic is replaced by the concrete and, when focused upon, poetic experience of the individual man crossing a bridge into a village. The Magnifico has undergone a change. He has wandered on stage a victim of his own metaphysics and has gone off with a heightened and intensified sense of the physical world—a sense which is the heart of the poetic sensibility.

In *Harmonium,* abstract thought is uncertain, an "old song that will not declare itself." The Magnifico of Stevens' earliest volume of poems is the man who focuses upon white walls and fruit trees, who chooses concrete, sensory experience over the uncertain buzzings of meditation and metaphysical musing.

Stevens employs two other techniques for presenting concrete experience in the pages of *Harmonium.* The first is the simple dramatic narrative, an approach which vanishes almost completely after "The Comedian as the Letter C." The other technique is one which, for want of a better term, I have labeled the "N Ways of Looking at an X" approach. Both of these techniques are effective methods of presenting external reality as a dynamic, creative process rather than as a fixed and static entity.

The long dramatic narrative entitled "The Comedian as the Letter C" has resisted effective scholarly analysis from its publication in 1923 until the present. Hi Simons has pointed out that from 1923 until 1940 the poem was the subject of eight "mutually contradictory" interpretations, none of them convincing enough to eliminate the others. Simons concludes that "their net effect is to cancel each other out." [9] Twenty-eight years of scholarship since 1940 have not appreciably altered the situation which Simons describes, though the explications of Eugene Nassar [10] and of Riddel [11] are worthy of attention. My purpose here is not so much to explicate "The Comedian as the Letter C" as to demonstrate the way in which Stevens uses external experience to create in Crispin a series of internal transformations.

[9] Simons, " 'The Comedian as the Letter C,' " p. 97.
[10] Nassar, *Wallace Stevens*, pp. 151–73.
[11] Riddel, *Clairvoyant Eye*, pp. 93–103.

It seems certain that Crispin undergoes three distinct transformations, three internal responses to three different sets of external conditions. In the first of these situations, Crispin, who has perhaps been over-proud, believer that man is the intelligence of his soil, finds that his "old mythology of self" has been "Blotched out beyond unblotching."

> Crispin
> The lutanist of fleas, the knave, the thane,
> The ribboned stick, the billowing breeches, cloak
> Of China, cap of Spain, imperative haw
> Of hum, inquisitorial botanist,
> And general lexicographer of mute
> And maidenly greenhorns, now beheld himself,
> A skinny sailor peering in the sea-glass.
>   (CP, p. 28)

The magnitude of the sea, the isolation from the environment of which he had presumed himself the intelligence, the suggestions of mortality which the sea may stir up, all combine to give Crispin a new view of himself. The greater accuracy of this view is suggested by the ability to go behind the "billowing breeches, cloak/ Of China, cap of Spain" and see that the sailor who wears them is "skinny," that he is forced to rely on a sea-glass, and, even with such man-contrived aid, is able to see no end to the waters which surround him. Here is a soil of which no man can claim to be "intelligence."

The imagery associated with the transformation in Crispin makes use of the archetypal pattern of death and rebirth, the pattern of the changing seasons.

> The salt hung on his spirit like a frost,
> The dead brine melted in him like a dew
> Of winter, until nothing of himself
> Remained, except some starker, barer self
> In a starker, barer world . . .

> Crispin
> Became an introspective voyager.
>
> (CP, p. 29)

The second transformation is also initiated by Crispin's encounter with a powerful natural phenomenon, in this case the "Thunderstorms of Yucatan." The passage invites comparison with Eliot's culminating section of *The Waste Land*, "What the Thunder Said." One of the themes employed by Eliot in that section is the approach to and ordeal of the Chapel Perilous where, in the Grail stories, the questing knight undergoes a night of supernatural terror before the achievement of his quest the next day.

Crispin, a partly purified questor of sorts, is an "annotator" at the beginning of *"Concerning the Thunderstorms of Yucatan."* He is concerned with the discovery of luxuriant life, with "trifles," and sees the cathedral "façade" only as an object for scholarly curiosity. But then the thunder speaks, and the wind "Came bluntly thundering, more terrible/ Than the revenge of music on bassoons" (CP, p. 32).

Crispin flees to the sanctuary of the cathedral and endures the storm there.

> He knelt in the cathedral with the rest,
> The connoisseur of elemental fate,
> Aware of exquisite thought. The storm was one
> Of many proclamations of the kind,
> Proclaiming something harsher than he learned
> From hearing signboards whimper in cold nights
> Or seeing the midsummer artifice
> Of heat upon his pane.
>
> (CP, pp. 32–33)

The thunder may make the vigil in the cathedral terrifying precisely because there is the suggestion that the supernatural does not exist. The whimpering signboard and the heated pane are lifeless and inanimate, empty of meaning; the thunder with its sound and fury brings the knowledge that the trifles of the opulent earth, the notes taken at the cabildo, the parrot squawks, all come to meaningless "boomings" when confronted with the "quintessential fact." Crispin finds that

> His mind was free
> And more than free, elate, intent, profound
> And studious of a self possessing him,
> That was not in him in the crusty town
> From which he sailed.
>
> (CP, p. 33)

This freedom and elation spring, I think, from the encounter with death, and they are parallel to the vision of our human condition as "unsponsored, free," set forth so beautifully in the concluding lines of "Sunday Morning."

The final transformation of the comedian takes place as he approaches Carolina, and once more it is "reality" which strikes the imagination and alters Crispin's "aesthetic."

> Tilting up his nose,
> He inhaled the rancid rosin, burly smells
> Of dampened lumber, emanations blown
> From warehouse doors, the gustiness of ropes,
> Decays of sacks, and all the arrant stinks
> That helped him round his rude aesthetic out.
> He savored rankness like a sensualist.
> He marked the marshy ground around the dock,
> The crawling railroad spur, the rotten fence,
> Curriculum for the marvelous sophomore.
> It purified. It made him see how much
> Of what he saw he never saw at all.
>
> (CP, p. 36)

Immediately following this encounter with ugly and decaying "reality," Crispin has been purified of his romantic notions and his overweening pride in man and man's imagination to the extent that he can reverse completely the note with which he began his voyage. "Nota: his soil is man's intelligence./ That's better. That's worth crossing seas to find" (CP, p. 36). Crispin has been humbled, has learned that poetry begins and ends in the affluence of the earth, and not in the poverty of man's spirit. Armed with that new knowledge, he casts off moonlight, founds a colony, marries, and has children. In short, Crispin becomes fruitful and creative as the result of the transformations he has undergone. The "general lexicographer of mute and maidenly greenhorns" has grown into a new role, that of father to daughters with curls.

As with the journey of the Magnifico, the end of Crispin's journeying is the discovery that external "reality," man's soil, is the source of creativity and the cause of man's internal change and growth.

In later volumes, Stevens meditates upon the relationship of the imagination and the phenomenal world; he knows that the mind is never satisfied and that the external world is in flux, and that consequently the relationship between the two is fluid, a thoroughly dynamic process involving two variables. In *Harmonium* Stevens does not discuss or meditate upon the dynamic nature of that relationship; rather he *presents* the ever-shifting relationship in concrete form. The metamorphoses of the phenomenal world and their entwinings with the transformations of the imagination are not the subject of the poem; they *are* the poem.

The two most familiar poems which present experience in this concrete form are "Sea Surface Full of Clouds" and "Thirteen Ways of Looking at a Blackbird." Each takes one aspect of reality, the first a sea surface at morning and the second a blackbird, and indicates both the constant changes that reality undergoes and the transformations which the mind makes in what the eye and ear perceive. Each is an open-ended poem; that is, the impressions which are set down serve as examples of a potentially endless number of such impressions. Although Stevens limits himself to thirteen ways of looking at a blackbird, the poem suggests that life is a potentially infinite series of encounters between an external, phenomenal "reality" which is forever changing and an imagination which can never be satisfied.

"Sea Surface Full of Clouds" has delighted critics, and scholars have pounced upon it with such fervor that I hesitate to add to the weight of critical attention which already threatens to be more than sufficient. I wish only to point out that the phenomenal universe in "Sea Surface" is presented as being in a state of process, a dynamic opposition of sea and sky which ends in reconciliation of some sort in the final lines of each section. David Ferry has pointed to another dimension of conflict in "Sea Surface Full of Clouds" in his observation that, in Stevens' poetry generally, "November, the sea, the ocean are all associated with 'bare reality.' Summer, umbrellas, and blue are often associated with the imagination." [12] Without in the least detracting from the correctness of Ferry's observation, M. L. Rosenthal points to a dramatic progression from section to section of the poem as well as within sections. Observing that the poem as a whole presents "five phases of the relationship between the observing, shaping human imagination and the 'objective' universe," Rosenthal examines the nature of that relationship as it moves from innocence through experience, culminating in the "reduction of the imagination to its most trivial status until its paradoxical restoration by external reality to 'transfiguring' glory." [13]

It may be worth adding to Rosenthal's notion of a progression within "Sea Surface Full of Clouds" that the final lines of each section present a movement from a separation of the sea of phenomenal reality and the sky and clouds of imagination toward a unity in which the two are "as one." In the first section the blue of heaven in the water is mere "antique reflection," a fairly literal presentation of the rela-

[12] Ferry, "Stevens' 'Sea Surface Full of Clouds.' "
[13] Rosenthal, "Stevens' 'Sea Surface Full of Clouds.' "

tionship between sea and sky. In section II the heaven is depicted as "spreading" colors on the sea, an act of covering which implies a separate coverer and covered. Section III has heaven "making" the sea petals blue, once again suggesting an act of creation, a doer and receiver of action. In the fourth section "the heaven rolled/ Its bluest sea-clouds in the thinking green." For the first time there is a merger, an almost sexual mingling of imagination and physical world. Even in this mixture, however, the two elements maintain separate identities. But in the final section

> the sea
> And heaven rolled as one and from the two
> Came fresh transfigurings of freshest blue.
>
> (CP, p. 102)

Here the heaven is not seen as "acting" on the sea, but the two roll "as one," and from the unified forces of physical sea and imagination come "fresh transfigurings of freshest blue." If one accepts Rosenthal's notion that the fifth section represents a reduction of the imagination to the most trivial status, the successful merger in that final section results from a turning outward, an acceptance of the primacy of the sea of "reality," the soil which is man's intelligence. Once again, *Harmonium* chooses the physical universe and its ability to stimulate the imagination.

"Thirteen Ways of Looking at a Blackbird" has suffered from its critics' tendency to fasten the blackbird to a single abstract meaning and make allegory of the entire poem. The primary association has been, as one might expect, that of the blackbird and death. Riddel, for example, speaks of the bird as a reminder of "death's ever-presence." [14] M. L. Rosenthal associates the blackbird with the paradoxical assertion of "Sunday Morning" that "Death is the mother of beauty." For him the blackbird is "a symbol of the insepara-

[14] Riddel, *Clairvoyant Eye,* p. 87.

bility of life and death in nature." [15] Peter McNamara agrees
with Rosenthal that the blackbird brings awareness of
death, but emphasizes that the awareness of death is "important . . . only as a stimulus to man's explorations of the
things of this life." [16] It is true enough that ravens, crows,
and other birds of black hue are often associated with
disaster and death in literature and in the popular imagination. Nevertheless, it seems to me that to see the blackbird
as representing death or any other single possibility from
all thirteen points of view is to misread the poem. As the
title implies, the point of "Thirteen Ways of Looking at a
Blackbird" is that in thirteen different contexts the imagination is able to provide thirteen different values for a bird
which would appear to the utilitarian or the scientist to
have only one value, one way of being looked at.

The dynamic character of the blackbird as symbol is
nowhere more apparent than in a comparison of stanzas I
and XIII, stanzas which function like bookends to hold the
poem together. The first stanza reads:

> Among twenty snowy mountains,
> The only moving thing
> Was the eye of the blackbird.
>
> (CP, p. 92)

The final stanza repeats the same motifs—the solitary and
silent blackbird against the equally silent emptiness of
white snow. The stanzas are similar enough to be thought
of as versions of a single scene. The difference, of course, is
that in stanza I the eye of the bird is seen as moving while
the snow is stationary. In stanza XIII, on the other hand,

> It was evening all afternoon.
> It was snowing

[15] Rosenthal, *The Modern Poets*, p. 128.
[16] McNamara, "The Multi-Faceted Blackbird and Wallace Stevens'
Poetic Vision," 446.

And it was going to snow.
The blackbird sat
In the cedar limbs.

(CP, p. 95)

Now the bird is motionless, but the white background is in motion, for the snow falls and "it was going to snow." In stanza I only the black dot at the center of the white poetic universe is mobile; in the last stanza, the black speck of the bird is the one stable point in a swirling and chaotic world of ever-moving white.

Thus, relative to the mountains surrounding it, the darting eye of the bird is "moving." However, relative to the falling snow, the blackbird is motionless on its cedar limb. Since, for Wallace Stevens, "Life Is Motion," the moving eye amid the lifeless mountains of the snowy desert place of stanza I would suggest life rather than death. The moving eye represents a conscious, watchful intelligence in an otherwise static and sterile universe.

Change the focus of the eye that views the bird, move it farther away perhaps, and the bird is without movement in a moving universe. The bird's eye can no longer be seen, but the bird can still be perceived, sitting in half-darkness in a cedar tree, a tree which traditionally provides the wood from which coffins are made. Rosenthal may be correct when he compares the bird's posture to that of Satan in *Paradise Lost* "when he flew up on the tree of Life in Eden and 'like a cormorant,' huge and evil, brooded over the whole doomed scene." [17] Here the blackbird does, indeed, seem to be a bird of evil omen, suggesting death and destruction. The poem opens with a blackbird which suggests a living presence at the center of a snowy waste land and ends with the same bird as a sinister, death-like presence in the midst of a universe of flux.

If the bird's range of symbolic values included only the

[17] Rosenthal, *The Modern Poets*, p. 129.

values of life and death, Rosenthal would be justified in viewing the bird as "a symbol of the inseparability of life and death in nature." However, in stanza II the character of the viewer intrudes and transforms the blackbird into a representative of disunity. "I was of three minds,/ Like a tree/ In which there are three blackbirds" (CP, p. 92). To the mind lacking inner harmony, the external world becomes emblematic of the mind's own fragmented condition.

To the different sort of viewer, however, the entire world is indivisibly one, not three. Given this insight,

> A man and a woman
> Are one.
> A man and a woman and a blackbird
> Are one.
> (CP, p. 93)

The stanza opens with a Christian cliché, a statement which has become the deadest of metaphors, and suddenly, by the inclusion of the blackbird, the entire stanza takes on new significance and vitality. "A man and a woman and a blackbird/ Are one" is simply a statement of fact uttered by a speaker of rather unusual perceptions, perhaps one who has freed himself from that conventional dualistic seeing which views the world as a series of multiplicities. There is no reason to speculate on the *meaning* of "A man and a woman and a blackbird/ Are one." It is enough to say that from the point of view of the speaker of stanza IV, the world is seen to be indivisibly monistic at first glance with an immediacy and clarity which we can only term rather inadequately to be "mystical." Stanza IV presents a quite remarkable way of looking at a blackbird, a way perhaps antithetical to the view of the blackbirds offered in stanza II.

There is a similar relationship between the significance of the blackbirds of stanza III and of stanza XII. The former is fairly logical and straightforward. "The blackbird whirled in the autumn winds./ It was a small part of the pantomime" (CP, p. 93). The bird, like the swirling leaves of autumn, is but a part in the pantomime of destruction, the seasonal tragedy, staged by the autumn winds. The reasoning man finds a pattern in the world, and in the pattern the bird has its part. No amount of reasoning or logic, however, can account for the insight of stanza XII. "The river is moving./ The blackbird must be flying" (CP, p. 94). Logically, the statement is simply nonsensical. The fact that the river is moving does not *of necessity* imply that the blackbird is flying as the verb form indicates that it does. We might easily reverse the saying, for the river doubtless will be flowing whether or not the blackbird is flying; but the juxtaposition of the two statements as Stevens has them suggests that the blackbird is the cause of movement, the source of eternal flux, and consequently, since life is motion, of life itself. We may infer from stanza XII that if the blackbird were not to fly, the rivers would cease their movements. This view of the blackbird seems to penetrate to a level at which it becomes, not part of the whole, but rather the dynamic force which moves the whole. It, and not the autumn wind, is the cause and end of movement.

Stanzas VIII and X invite comparison because they demonstrate the blackbird's significance to two kinds of poet.

> I know noble accents
> And lucid, inescapable rhythms;
> But I know, too,
> That the blackbird is involved
> In what I know.
>   (CP, p. 94)

Stevens as poet knows that technique alone, mastery of accents and rhythm, does not result in poetry. Here the use of the blackbird appears to be a form of synecdoche in which the bird represents the physical affluence of the planet of which the poet sings. The bird's power is such that Stevens insists,

> At the sight of blackbirds
> Flying in a green light,
> Even the bawds of euphony
> Would cry out sharply.
>
> (CP, p. 94)

I take the "bawds of euphony" to be poets of an inferior grade, those who have mastered rhythm and accent, but whose pleasing sounds lack meaning because they have no deep feeling for the beauties and joys of this life, this earth. The beauty of the blackbirds in a green light could startle the "bawds" into crying out "sharply," a spontaneous cry very different from the euphonious sounds which they usually produce. If the blackbird comes to be involved in what they know, these "bawds" may cease their bawdiness and become true poets.

Stanza IX, "When the blackbird flew out of sight,/ It marked the edge/ Of one of many circles," uses the blackbird to symbolize our myriad human limitations, our horizons, and the kinship which the physical universe, represented by the bird, creates among human beings. The bird joins every human being within whose circle of vision he flies.

If the blackbird is an emblem of beauty in stanza X, it becomes a cause for fear to the nervous rider across Connecticut in stanza XI. Richard Ellman points out that the view of the man in the glass coach is distorted. It is as unusual a vision in its way as is the "mystical" vision of stanza IV. Glass, Ellman notes, is almost always a bar to sight for Stevens; moreover the man has *not* seen the blackbird, but only "his own dark mind, the shadow of his equipage." [18]

[18] Ellman, "Wallace Stevens' Ice Cream," 103.

The blackbird also seems to cause fear to the viewer in stanza VI. Perhaps the "to and fro" motion of the blackbird's shadow on the "barbaric glass" reminds the watcher of the movement of a pendulum, of the inexorability of time. This resemblance, coupled with the starkness of the winter scene, might help explain the cause of the "mood" which "traced in the shadow/ An indecipherable cause."

The pivotal stanza VII of the poem uses the blackbird in opposition to imaginary golden birds.

> O thin men of Haddam,
> Why do you imagine golden birds?
> Do you not see how the blackbird
> Walks around the feet
> Of the women about you?
> (CP, p. 93)

Thinness in Stevens usually represents concern with the wrong kind of knowledge, knowledge in the abstract rather than in the particular. Whereas "fat" Jocundus has no capacity for imaginative creation, the "thin-nosed" hidalgo of "A Thought Revolved" is one who longs for a world of pure imagination, a world free from "beggars wet with dew" and from dogs howling "at barren bone." The golden birds imagined by the thin men remind one of the birds of Yeats' Byzantium, that world of artifice and permanence; the blackbirds at the feet of the women suggest the joys which belong to the "young in one another's arms."

It is this blackbird, perhaps, this bird of earth, beautiful and suggesting earthly joys, which best characterizes the world of *Harmonium*. Wordsworth looks back to his Eden as he remembers it, and the Ancient Mariner remembers the joy with which his crew-mates put out to sea, but Stevens' presentation of Eden is, for the most part, an unmeditated and unmeditated upon celebration of the sun and its delights. It is a poetry in which "meadow, grove, and stream/ The earth, and every common sight" has not totally lost its "celestial light," although for Stevens the "celestial light" that counts is that of the sun which is the "savage source" of life on our planet. Stevens needs no joy beyond that of earth; for the *Harmonium* years at least, the sun is ample, and will suffice.

Ideas of Order

When amorists, even amorists enamored of the sun, grow bald, and when the sun itself seems, perhaps from over-familiarity, to fade, the precarious relationship between lover's eye and beloved sun requires what a marriage counsellor might term "a period of adjustment." Such a period is chronicled in Stevens' 1936 volume of poems, *Ideas of Order*. The volume is transitional, not only in style but also in substance; in *Ideas of Order* Stevens begins to move from a poetry of almost pure sensory experience to a poetry of reflection and meditation. Even the title suggests this internalization, for it suggests that the poems of Stevens' second volume will deal with "Ideas." The "Ideas" are there, but Stevens is nevertheless more likely at this stage in his career to discover an "Order" in the chaos of experience than he is to *impose* an order upon that chaos by the power of his imagination.

In this volume Stevens is still concerned with external experience, but his principle concern is now with social and political experience rather than with the limited and personal sensory delights of *Harmonium*. Hoon has vanished, and he has been replaced by swarms of political men, cold men for whom the sun shines fitfully, if it shines at all. The voices which endure from the *Harmonium* period are the tired voices of Don Joost and the monocled uncle. Both have warned of a fading of the sun, and the fulfillment of their prophecies can be seen in *Ideas of Order*. The dominant mood of the volume is a sense of things falling back to coldness, of the autumnal departure of the cosmic energy of the sun. Turning from the sun to man as a subject for poetry, Stevens finds the world to be "bad, sad, and mad."

Ideas of Order begins with "Farewell to Florida," a poetic assertion of change. The images of transformation are inescapable. The journey, the assertion that "the past is dead," the image of the shed snakeskin, and the image of the deserted house all combine to indicate that the poet-narrator is leaving more than Florida behind in his "Farewell." He is leaving a vivid, beautiful land composed half of sun, half of sand. The South which the poet leaves is a land fundamentally without motion or change, while the dominant characteristic of the North to which he sails is the turbulent movement of men in crowds. The imagery associated with Florida is beautiful, but it is imagery of rust and bones, dung and death. That which is motionless, unused, turns rusty, while that which is moving is living, even when the motion takes place in crowds. Perhaps Stevens is suggesting that a life extolling purely sensory experience, a life without shadows, cannot be long endured, for the ground in shadowless Florida is "ashen," and the wind from the north whistles in "in a sepulchral South" (CP, p. 117). Eugene Nassar insists that "Perhaps the basic dichotomy between the North and South in Stevens' mind is that in the North one is in twentieth-century society, while in the South one is more alone with chaotic, exotic reality." [1] Although Nassar uses "reality" carelessly, and although it is questionable that the life of the North is any less chaotic than that of the South, it seems certain that the journey northward from Florida does represent a change from the

---

[1] Nassar, *Wallace Stevens*, p. 40.

experience of the individual with the sun to the historical and social experience of the individual with his fellow man.

The tension in "Farewell to Florida" is a familiar one; in "escaping" to the North the narrator has escaped the dangers of the beautiful, peaceful, and utterly destructive womb and has accepted the responsibility that is expressed in movement, in being alive. He chooses to return to the society of men, knowing full well that their needs will "bind [him] round" (CP, p. 118). As is so often the case in American poetry, Paul Bunyan is pitted against Rip Van Winkle, and in "Farewell to Florida" the needs of a world of men, the promises to be kept, win out over the desire for the peace represented by "the vivid blooms, . . . the rust and bones" (CP, p. 118).

Nevertheless, the North to which the poet journeys is "leafless and lies in a wintry slime/ Both of men and clouds, a slime of men in crowds" (CP, p. 118). It is a land of "macabre mice," of evenings "without angels," of "fading sun," and of "gray stones and gray pigeons." It is a world for the most part cheerless, dark and deadly, a "panorama of despair" which includes the nigger cemetery and the volcano, the gallant chateau with empty bed, and the boarded and bare hotels with broken columns.

The thirties were a difficult time for Stevens, for the social moods and changes of the time were indeed "alien" to him. Stevens' dissatisfaction is in part that of a man in an uncomfortable period of transition, for he is now a poet in search of a subject. His reward for his new concern with order, man and society seems at first to be entirely negative. He has escaped the pleasant dangers of rusting away in Florida only to arrive in a North that threatens to freeze him to death, a world without a vital sun. It is true that the sun appears and is compared to Walt Whitman, certainly a hearty enough figure, in the poem entitled "Like Decorations in a Nigger Cemetery," but it is a sun of autumn that appears, a sun that is "passing." The sense of autumnal chill is pervasive throughout the poem, and although there is indeed sun and motion above the nigger cemetery, the effect is far from that of the bright, intense sun of *Harmonium:*

> The sun of Asia creeps above the horizon
> Into this haggard and tenuous air,
> A tiger lamed by nothingness and frost.
>
> (CP, p. 153)

In place of the sun, *Ideas of Order* offers a new image which becomes an integral part of Stevens' poetic world—that of the rock. The journey from Florida to the North is repeated in "How to Live. What to Do," a poem short enough to cite in its entirety.

> Last evening the moon rose above this rock
> Impure upon a world unpurged.
> The man and his companion stopped
> To rest before the heroic height.
>
> Coldly the wind fell upon them
> In many majesties of sound:
> They that had left the flame-freaked sun
> To seek a sun of fuller fire.
>
> Instead there was this tufted rock
> Massively rising high and bare
> Beyond all trees, the ridges thrown
> Like giant arms among the clouds.
>
> There was neither voice nor crested image,
> No chorister, nor priest. There was
> Only the great height of the rock
> And the two of them standing still to rest.
>
> There was the cold wind and the sound
> It made, away from the muck of the land
> That they had left, heroic sound
> Joyous and jubilant and sure.
>
> (CP, pp. 125–26)

The man and his companion are travelers in an unpurged world, a world like that of Stevens' North where the men of "violent minds" and their chaotic milling about represent the less pleasant aspects of twentieth-century life. If the world of *Harmonium* is an Edenic place of innocence and harmony, Ralph J. Mills, Jr. has made an appropriate assertion about the world of *Ideas of Order*. Mills says that the man and his companion "more than suggest Adam and Eve cast from the Garden of Eden." The rock, that which must replace the sun, is treated with awe and respect, and the poet's mention of the absence of chorister and priest indicates that the outward trappings of religious ceremony are not needed to quicken the feelings of religious experience. Mills believes that there is in the implied attitude toward the rock a mixture of "a primitive pantheism and an empiricist's recognition of the definite and physical, both circumscribed by the poet's mind." [2]

Stevens realizes the need of the twentieth-century man to free himself from the "muck of the land" if he is to come to something sure. Stevens' man and his companion find that what is "sure" in their unpurged world is not the blazing sun, but the sombre shade of the giant rock. If the rock is without warmth, at least it is certain (or so it seems in *Ideas of Order*) and it has heroic stature. The wanderers from the Eden of *Harmonium* find that the wind blowing over the rock produces a "heroic sound/ Joyous and jubilant and sure" (CP, p. 126). Thus, although the rock replaces the sun, and the colors of *Harmonium* diminish and deepen, the seeker of an answer to the question of "How to Live. What to Do" finds the answer by turning from the sludge of twentieth-century society and finding the basic slate. The wind for Stevens, as for earlier romantic poets, may function as a symbol for poetic inspiration, and if it does, it is significant that Stevens replaces the conventional

[2] Mills, "Wallace Stevens: The Image of the Rock," p. 97.

Aeolian harp with the tufted rock that represents something akin to reality in *Ideas of Order*. Only after a man and his companion discover that which is most certain, most sure, does the wind fall upon them "In many majesties of sound." The world for Stevens is not so vivid and not so warm as it once was, but reality is still to be sought in the external world, is still thought of as being discoverable, and, once discovered, is still a fixed quality, stable and sure.

Despite the possibility of raising poetry out of the slime of the Northern waste to which Stevens has journeyed, *Ideas of Order* is a volume relatively retrospective in tone. Over and over the poet speaks of the change that has taken place in his relationship with the physical universe. In "The Sun this March," he tells us

> The exceeding brightness of this early sun
> Makes me conceive how dark I have become,
>
> And re-illumines things that used to turn
> To gold in broadest blue . . .
>
> (CP, p. 133)

In "Anglais Mort a Florence," the hero is one for whom "A little less returned . . . each spring." Like the poet of *Harmonium*, the Englishman in Florence

> remembered the time when he stood alone,
> When to be and delight to be seemed to be one,
> Before the colors deepened and grew small.
>
> (CP, p. 149)

In "Autumn Refrain" the sense of loss and desolation is inescapable.

> The skreak and skritter of evening gone
> And grackles gone and sorrows of the sun,
> The sorrows of sun, too, gone . . .
>
> (CP, p. 160)

When the sun rises on this wasteland, it is dull and without cheer.

Melodious skeletons, for all of last night's music
Today is today and the dancing is done.

Dew lies on the instruments of straw that you were playing,
The ruts in your empty road are red.

(CP, p. 160)

Although the mind may discover a "force" inherent in the rising sun, Stevens dolefully admits that "The mind is smaller than the eye," and the eye looks at the clouds and foretells a swampy rain. Even when the light falls felicitously, as at twilight in the poem called "Delightful Evening," the poet finds in the slant of light reason enough for internal hurt. The twilight is, he discovers, "overfull/ Of wormy metaphors" (CP, p. 162). Man no longer finds delight merely in "being" in the world of Stevens' second volume; instead he finds himself more and more returning to Eden in memory, for he cannot return in any other way.

Although the climate of *Harmonium* has, Stevens assures us, vanished along with the past, Stevens is far from comfortable in the new dispensation. He is more acutely conscious than ever of his alienation, of the separation of the romantic from the men in swarms. The poem "Sailing after Lunch" is, according to Joseph Riddel, "the voice of *Harmonium* hesitantly raised against the forces of history." [3] The appraisal is accurate, except that it does not take into account the ironic, self-mocking tone which Stevens employs to express his theme. The poet of *Harmonium* is a part of the dead past, and his voice is to be regarded only ironically; nevertheless, Stevens is not satisfied with his new Northern climate. As Daniel Fuchs says, "The title evokes that precarious sinking feeling familiar to modern writers since Baudelaire remarked on the immense nausea of the billboards." [4] "Sailing after Lunch" seems to me to be a rather wistful and uncertain attempt to reconcile the

[3] Riddel, *Clairvoyant Eye*, p. 120.
[4] Fuchs, *The Comic Spirit of Wallace Stevens*, p. 109.

heavy and dirty "historical sail" with the poetic imagination, a feat which Stevens feels can be performed only by one who is willing to "expunge all people" (CP, p. 121). He knows that he cannot return to the world of *Harmonium* (the sailboat will not make Florida), that "the romantic must never remain, . . ./ and must never again return" (CP, p. 120), but at the same time he affirms that the self, simply the way one feels, may give "That slight transcendence" to the dirty sail of history. The reconciliation of social and historical concerns with the powers of the poetic craft forms a most delicate balance. Surely the bright rush through the summer air that concludes the poem has an element of forced gaiety about it, and the dominant impression left by "Sailing After Lunch" is Stevens' sense of his role as "A most inappropriate man/ In a most unpropitious place" (CP, p. 120).

The theme of alienation, of the poet's acute discomfiture in his new environment, is inescapable in the pages of *Ideas of Order*. In "Mozart, 1935," the artist is confronted by a mob of angry men who throw stones upon the roof while he tries to practice arpeggios. Stevens' feelings about the age in which he finds himself are suggested in the opening stanza.

> Poet, be seated at the piano.
> Play the present, its hoo-hoo-hoo
> Its shoo-shoo-shoo, its ric-a-nic,
> Its envious cachinnation.
>
> (CP, p. 131)

Once again, the poem is an attempt to reconcile the discordance of the unpropitious time and place in which the poet finds himself with the poetic need to be the voice of his age, however much that voice must be the expression of "angry fear" or of "besieging pain." The poem suggests that the voice of the poet can help man endure, for it is in "that wintry sound" that "sorrow is released,/ Dismissed, absolved/ In a starry placating" (CP, p. 132).

The botanist on the alp, a dramatic mask for the contemplative and alienated man, is also discontent.

> Panoramas are not what they used to be.
> Claude has been dead a long time
> And apostrophes are forbidden on the funicular.
> Marx has ruined Nature,
> For the moment.
>> (CP, p. 134)

We find in the complaint of the botanist the central problem with which *Ideas of Order* is concerned. The modern world of swarming men is without a central composition, without a theme, without an order. The botanist is nevertheless able to make an affirmation, an assertion that "the panorama of despair/ Cannot be the specialty/ Of this ecstatic air" (CP, p. 135). In "Botanist on Alp (No. 2)" the narrator suggests a possible way of finding meaning in the seeming chaos of dogmatic Marxism and of dogmatic Christianity. Once again, poetry seems to be the answer.

> Chant, O ye faithful, in your paths
> The poem of long celestial death;
>
> For who could tolerate the earth
> Without that poem or without
>
> An earthier one, tum, tum-ti-tum,
> As of those crosses, glittering,
>
> And merely of their glittering,
> A mirror of a mere delight?
>> (CP, p. 136)

As in "Sunday Morning," we are reminded that death is the mother of beauty, and that the glittering things of the earth are delightful and sufficient in and of themselves. The cross is no answer to despair for Stevens when it is viewed as a symbol, but when it is seen as simply one of the bright things of the earth which the sun gilds as it falls upon them, it becomes a source of delight. The botanist offers an affirmation in the face of despair, but the affirmation is a "mere" one, a rather unsatisfactory "tum, tum-ti-tum."

"A Fading of the Sun" is an effective restatement of the poet's difficulty in adjusting to his new commitment to the world of men and history.

> Who can think of the sun costuming clouds
> When all people are shaken
> Or of night endazzled, proud,
> When people awaken
> And cry and cry for help?
>
> (CP, p. 139)

Harmonium was, at its best, a book of "sun costuming clouds." The figure is especially apt in Stevens' symbolic mythology, for clouds, as we have seen, suggest the imagination for him, while the sun stands for the intense brilliance of the phenomenal world. The combination of the two is beautiful, but the creations of sun and clouds are unthinkable in a land of suffering like that of the poet of *Ideas of Order*. Stevens insists, as he does throughout *Ideas of Order*, that truth is discoverable, if man will allow himself to search for it on this earth. If one does away with the notions of solace to be found "within a book," specifically a book such as the *Bible*, if nothing is divine, then all things are divine, and with this knowledge man discovers that

> The tea,
> The wine is good. The bread,
> The meat is sweet.
> And they will not die.
>
> (CP, p. 139)

Like the crosses of the botanist, the bread and wine become sweet; they provide a way out of the despair which modern man feels as soon as they yield their symbolic significance and are accepted as merely being among the good and enduring things of the earth. Actual wine, actual bread, the stuff of earth, will not die; on the other hand, the mythology of the bread and wine had become, in Stevens' eyes, moribund. As in *Harmonium,* Stevens insists upon joy in the physical universe; however, the poet of *Ideas of Order* has heard the cries of mankind and knows that for his age, "The tea is bad, bread sad" (CP, p. 139). One suspects that Stevens is slightly uncomfortable with the solutions of the botanist and the narrative voice of "A Fading of the Sun." They represent the best that *Harmonium* has had to offer, but the sweetness of the external world of things may not be sufficient comfort in the cold and darkening world of *Ideas of Order.*

The difference between Florida and the North is, as Stevens puts it in "Academic Discourse at Havana," that "the sustenance of the wilderness/ Does not sustain us in the metropoles" (CP, p. 142). Again, much of the poem is devoted to the expression of a sense of loss, of things falling back to coldness.

> Life is an old casino in a park.
> The bills of the swans are flat upon the ground.
> A most desolate wind has chilled Rouge-Fatima
> And a grand decadence settles down like cold.
>
> (CP, p. 142)

Like the hotel that is Europe in "Botanist on Alp (No. 1)," the casino of modern life has "boarded windows," and the rain which sweeps through those windows and the leaves which fill the casino's fountains suggest decadence and disorder. All of this has come about, Stevens suggests, because

> Politic man ordained
> Imagination as the fateful sin.
> Grandmother and her basketful of pears
> Must be the crux for our compendia.
>
> (CP, p. 143)

Grandmother and her pears, sentimental subjects dear to the "burgher's breast," have replaced the ripe and lusty myth which Stevens declares was once "more fruitful than the weeks/ Of ripest summer, . . ." (CP, p. 143). The problem is the constant one of *Ideas of Order*. What is the function of the creative man, the poet, in a world of burghers? Stevens' answer seems to be that his role is more vital than ever.

> let the poet on his balcony
> Speak and the sleepers in their sleep shall move,
> Waken, and watch the moonlight on their floors.
> This may be benediction, sepulcher,
> And epitaph. It may, however, be
> An incantation that the moon defines
> By mere example opulently clear.
>
> (CP, pp. 144–45)

An "incantation," a spell or charm for warding off evil, is exactly what a world infected with a grand malady needs; for Stevens, the poet is the figure most likely to provide the proper words to cure the human spirit.

Just as such *Harmonium* poems as "Le Monocle de Mon Oncle" seem to anticipate in mood the fading sun of *Ideas of Order*, there are moments in Stevens' second volume when he returns in spirit, or in memory, to the Florida he thought he had left behind forever. Such a moment is crystallized in the poem called "The Idea of Order at Key West." Stevens asserts that the mind's rage to establish an order can, at least momentarily, master the chaos of reality.

As one expects from Stevens, the ordering principle in a disordered universe turns out to be the spirit of poetry. Stevens' poetic genius of the shore is much like other images of the poetic imagination which have been created by various romantic poets. One thinks, for example, of Keats's Lamia or the damsel with a dulcimer of Coleridge's "Kubla Khan." Like Lamia and the Abyssinian maid, Stevens' nameless maid has strange powers, is mysterious in origin, and is a kind of creator or artisan. The complete absence of physical description, the uncertainty which surrounds her, the ambiguous nature of Stevens' perception of her, all combine to leave us with a figure as wraith-like as the products of our dreams.

The fact that Florida is the setting of "The Idea of Order at Key West," rather than the North of men moving in crowds, indicates that the poem is not typical of a volume which opens with "Farewell to Florida." The poet-narrator discovers that the nameless singer makes a world with her song, and, when the singing ends, discovers that as he returns to the town the world appears different to him. The entry into the fictive world of the song provides an ordering principle which remains, even when the song has ended. Like Keats after the departure of the nightingale or after his return from the imaginary world of the Grecian urn, Stevens is changed by his experience. The ordering of the sea is his own version of Keats's " 'Beauty is truth, truth beauty,' —that is all/ Ye know on earth, and all ye need to know." Both poets have learned that the beauty of order leads to insight, to a valid perception of what might be called "reality."

The "idea of order" which Stevens has at Key West is not an "idea of order" which will suffice for him in his new environment. The entire tone of the poem is one of reminiscence, a remembrance of things past in which the verb tenses which describe the ordering experiences are entirely in the past. Only the address to Ramon Fernandez has the immediacy of present tense, of direct address. The poem is similar in tone to many of the other works in *Ideas of Order* in that it represents the poignancy of Stevens' sense of loss of a meaningful relationship between himself and the natural world. Ramon Fernandez has no answer to Stevens' query.

> Ramon Fernandez, tell me, if you know,
> Why, when the singing ended and we turned
> Toward the town, tell why the glassy lights,
> The lights in the fishing boats at anchor there,

> As the night descended, tilting in the air,
> Mastered the night and portioned out the sea,
> Fixing emblazoned zones and fiery poles,
> Arranging, deepening, enchanting night.
>
> (CP, p. 130)

The sole possible answer seems to be the one Stevens him-self provides, that of the mind's insatiable desire to establish order, "the blessed rage" that arranges even "words of the sea." The "idea of order" in Florida's keys is quite different from the idea of order in such poems as "The Pleasures of Merely Circulating." "The Pleasures of Merely Circulating" views "being" as constant flux; life, once again, is motion. In *Harmonium*, however, the celebration of life and motion is that of a marriage, and the central mystery around which the dance-like movement goes on is the phallic stump, itself immovable, but suggestive of the life force. In "The Pleasures of Merely Circulating" the motion swirls around the central stanza which celebrates the mystery of death.

> Is there any secret in skulls,
> The cattle skulls in the woods?
> Do the drummers in black hoods
> Rumble anything out of their drums?
>
> (CP, p. 150)

The answer, quite obviously, is "no." Death has no secrets; it is absolute and without meaning. The final "meaning" of all the motion that is life is that such motion is mere chaos. "Mrs. Anderson's Swedish baby/ Might well have been German or Spanish," since all ends in death, and there is no secret in skulls, whether those skulls be of cattle, Swedes, Germans, or Spaniards.

The sombre overtones of "The Pleasures of Merely Circulating" are much more in keeping with the atmosphere of *Ideas of Order* than the moment of perceived order at Key West. The moments of ecstatic encounters of the mind with the phenomenal world occur only occasionally in the slime of the North. The Stevens of *Ideas of Order* is much more aware than was the Stevens of *Harmonium* of the inexorable ticking of the clock; out of his new awareness grows what seems to be a new notion of the poet's relationship to humanity.

Union of the weakest develops strength
Not wisdom. Can all men, together, avenge
One of the leaves that have fallen in autumn?
But the wise man avenges by building his city in snow.

(CP, p. 158)

Men in swarms, men dealing from the contorted strength of society, are powerless against the forces of time and decay. Nonetheless, the poet creates out of the material that he has at his command the romantic tenements of snow and ice which, being sufficient, will help men endure.

The fitful twilight of *Ideas of Order* is indeed aswarm with "wormy metaphors." In turning to society as a subject for poetry, Stevens has discovered the depth of his alienation as poet and thinker; moreover, discontented with the swarms of men of the North, he feels acutely the loss of the purely sensory delights of sun and bright fruit and cockatoos which were so much a part of the *Harmonium* experience. The colors have faded, and the "harmony" of which he was once a part has given way to an "idea" of an order which is perceived only vaguely and which gives scant comfort.

The Man with the Blue Guitar

The fading sunlight of *Ideas of Order* illumines a kind of poetic cul-de-sac. The "felicitous eve," when all is said and done, is found to be "overfull of wormy metaphors," and Stevens learns that the celebrator of the sun is at a loss when sun and senses begin to fade. Thus, *Ideas of Order* presents a problem which Stevens must solve if he is to continue to write poetry. The problem is basic—if it is not enough merely to sing hymns to the beauty of the phenomenal world, the poet must discover for himself the proper role of the artist in modern society.

Stevens was already working on his answer when *Ideas of Order* came out, and that answer took the form of two short volumes of poetry—*Owl's Clover* and *The Man with the Blue Guitar*. The two have much in common, for both are the sort of exercises in which Stevens was able to give "prolonged attention to a single subject," [1] as he once wrote Harriet Monroe he wanted to do. Both are topical, and both are attempts to engage his poetic imagination with the contemporaneous; both are intellectual, increasingly meditative, and yet both have as their subjects the actuality of

[1] Stevens, *Letters*, p. 230.

48

American life in the 1930's. Both are intellectual lyrics, and an examination of their lines of argument is useful to an understanding of Stevens' development.

Owl's Clover is a volume of five long, closely related poems concerning the effect of the depression on artistic creativity. The first of the five poems, "The Old Woman and the Statue" is a confrontation of the suffering, poverty, and despair of the times by the imaginative work of a more tranquil time. The old woman modifies the present, and at the same time she illustrates the failures of the forms of the past to cope with the physical and spiritual poverty of the depression era. The statue becomes a figure for any outmoded and rigid order, whether artistic, religious, or political. The rigidity of the statue renders it obsolete in the midst of change; it is meaningless to the old woman.

The second poem of *Owl's Clover,* "Mr. Burnshaw and the Statue," is a defense of poetry, of the poet's politics, in the face of an attack by Marxist critic Stanley Burnshaw. Stevens rejects the rigid order of the future, the Marxian Utopia, as firmly as he had rejected the order of the past in "The Old Woman and the Statue." In its place he offers individual acceptance of change and chaos, the continual rebirths of the self which make the present the only reality and all concepts of the future mere fictions.

"The Greenest Continent" is set in Africa and juxtaposes the American statue and the chaotic despair which surrounds it with the vital, passionate, dark, and irrational world of the African jungle. The poem introduces "Fatal Ananke," the "common god," who seems to be a figure for the most elemental human passions and desires. Ananke is a kind of archetypal force, perhaps that force which Stevens elsewhere describes as man's "blessed rage for order." The false orders of past and future have been swept away, and Stevens has plunged into the heart of darkness to come to elemental reality, reality which can be presented in a vital form. Ananke "caused the statue to be made/ And he shall fix the place where it will stand" (OP, p. 60). The African statue is far different from the Old Woman's. The American statue is "imagined in the cold," and stands "among/ The common-places of which it formed a part" (OP, pp. 56–57). The statue on the "greenest continent" stands amid "drenching reds, the dark/ And drenching crimsons" (OP, p. 57), and, as always in Stevens, red is the color of harshest, most elemental reality.

The fourth poem of *Owl's Clover,* "A Duck for Dinner," presents the figure of the "Bulgar" as representative of the American immigrant and juxtaposes him with the burk-skinned "crosser of snowy divides" who seems to represent the moribund ideal of the American adventurer. The Bulgar suggests the rise of the workers, and something of Stevens' discontent with his decade may be seen in the fact that he sees the workers' rise as taking place "an inch at a time." For him the rise of the working classes is a matter of a gradually evolving growth of sensitivity, the slow creation of a head which at last may come to speak, though the voice will be a "grizzled" one. The poem ends darkly, with a cluster of images and unanswered, unanswerable questions which make up Stevens' vision of the wasteland.

> How shall we face the edge of time? We walk
> In the park. We regret we have no nightingale.
> We must have the throstle on the gramophone.
> Where shall we find more than derisive words?
> When shall lush chorals spiral through our fire
> And daunt that old assassin, heart's desire?
>
> (OP, p. 66)

The final mood of "A Duck for Dinner" leads naturally to the fifth poem, "Sombre Figuration." The poem introduces a "subman," a kind of archetypal figure who

> was born within us as a second self,
> A self of parents who have never died,

Whose lives return, simply, upon our lips,
Their words and ours . . .

(OP, p. 67)

The "subman" is closely related to Ananke, for he also is elemental, vital, and irrational. He is the force which can surprise the "sterile rationalist," and he is the source of images, of "Maidens in bloom, bulls under sea" (OP, p. 67). He is also an early form of the hero-poet who is to be "man number one" in "The Man with the Blue Guitar," but he is a much less successfully presented figure. As representative of our vital being, the "sprawling portent" leads us to a commitment to spontaneous, elemental life, to "a passion merely to be/ For the gaudium of being . . ." (OP, p. 71). As in "The Greenest Continent," Stevens' answer to the malaise of his time seems to be his own form of collectivism, that of the creative energies of the collective unconscious. Apparently, it is not an answer which wears well so far as Stevens is concerned, for *Owl's Clover*, for all its length and its elevated subject matter, is omitted from *The Collected Poems*.[2]

The exclusion of *Owl's Clover* from "The Whole of Harmonium" is interesting; Stevens seems to have been troubled with the poem almost from its completion. As early as October, 1935, Stevens wrote Ronald Lane Latimer that

> The poem is a source of a good deal of trouble to me at the moment, because, having purposely used a good many stock figures (what is now called *Victorian ideology*) it seems most un-Burnshawesque. I cannot tell what I shall do about it until I have tinkered with it a bit; it may be better to leave it as it is. . . . my principal concern with this poem (and, I suppose with any poem) is not so much with the ideas as with the poetry of the thing . . . I don't have ideas that are permanently fixed. My conception of

---

[2] Surely the most authoritative comments on *Owl's Clover* are Stevens' own, and the critic should see his series of letters to Hi Simons on the "statue poems." *Letters,* pp. 366–75.

what a poet should be and do changes, and I hope, constantly grows.[3]

There may be a clue in this letter which indicates that something more than "rhetoric" was responsible for Stevens' ultimate dismissal of *Owl's Clover* from his *Collected Poems*. The poem is held together, as Joseph Riddel observes, by "the order of its *idee fixé* and the urgency which compelled Stevens to write it." [4] In responding to the fixed idea which was Burnshaw's, Stevens had fallen into too great a concern with the idea and too little a concern with the poetry of the work. Stevens finds himself on the defensive, attacking another man's world view rather than setting forth his own. The difference between *The Man with the Blue Guitar* and *Owl's Clover* is that *Blue Guitar* manages to turn abstract ideas and topical and personal allusions into the concrete and universal stuff of poetry. Both poems represent Stevens' turning to the intellectual lyric mode which was to mark his style from 1937 on, but in *Owl's Clover* Stevens has tried to argue rather than create, and the result is the failure which Stevens himself cites, that of "rhetoric." Frank Kermode says, "one sees what Stevens meant by using the term 'rhetoric' pejoratively here; there is much random noise, the dry clatter of uninterestingly queer diction and stiff rhythms." [5] I suspect that the uncharacteristic "random noise," "queer diction," and "stiff rhythms" are those of a poet experimenting with a new mode, a poetry of ideas.

"The Man with the Blue Guitar" is, as noted earlier, also an intellectual lyric poem, but this time Stevens is more successful in setting forth answers to the questions which *Ideas of Order* and the chaos of the thirties had raised. It is in "The Man with the Blue Guitar" that Stevens begins his

[3] Stevens, *Letters*, p. 289.
[4] Riddel, *Clairvoyant Eye*, p. 123.
[5] Kermode, *Wallace Stevens*, p. 64.

search for a myth in which the poem as the act of the mind might replace the outworn religious myths which would no longer suffice.

"The Man with the Blue Guitar" consists of thirty-three fragmentary and loosely related meditative poems. Unlike "The Comedian as the Letter C," the *Harmonium* poem of comparable length, "The Man with the Blue Guitar" does not employ the chronological structure of the dramatic narrative. Even the introspective, musing voice of the narrator of "Farewell to Florida" has been abandoned, perhaps because it is too conscious of itself, too much the rhetorical form of a performer speaking to an audience. In "The Man with the Blue Guitar" the conscious, logical order of *Harmonium* and *Ideas of Order* is replaced by the ebb and flow of a kind of free association, the activity of a mind meditating freely, plumbing the depths of its various "pools" of thought. Consequently, there is a constant shifting of person, of tense, of mood, of subject, of degree of impressionism from poem to poem with "Blue Guitar."

The poem opens with a dialog, an exchange between "The man" and "They." In section II "The man" has become "I" and the others have disappeared. By section V the plural group of section I has apparently returned to insist that the shearsman "not speak to us of the greatness of poetry," although by this time Stevens is no longer using quotation marks to indicate changes from one speaker to another. It is as if he begins with an external, dramatic mode, not too different, after all, from the dramatic dialog form of "Sunday Morning," but drops the form almost immediately and accepts both voices as aspects of a single meditation. The dropping of the opening debate and the refusal to be confined to a single setting—even so vague a one as the "green day"—represent a rejection of the presentation of the tension of external conflict and a turning instead toward a presentation of a conflict of opposed symbols and values existing within the mind.

The shearsman, a strummer of the blue guitar, is a dramatic figure, but one quite different from those Stevens employed in *Harmonium*. Don Joost and Hoon, Azcan and the inchling, the Magnifico and the Cuban Doctor, all represent individual world views, and Stevens used such figures to probe various extremes in methods of perceiving and interpreting reality. The blue guitar player, on the other hand, is a figure for the creative, imaginative artist-craftsman. As such, he is less limited than were the figures of *Harmonium;* his meditations are the substance of the poem, and they represent the groping of creative man to find a myth that will serve for our time. Although the "shearsman" is "he" in the first section of the poem, and we know of him only what he says and what he does, as the poem progresses we become party to the workings of his mind and his imagination as they move rapidly over the various images, motifs, and moods that make up "The Man with the Blue Guitar." The thoughts of the blue guitar player are much less consciously ordered than are those of the monologists of *Harmonium*. The views of Hoon or Crispin were either whole and direct and constant or else were logical responses to the external world, to events. On the other hand, the shearsman follows no pattern except the random paths of his own meditative associations. He encompasses both Hoon and Crispin, and he has learned much from the experiences of each.

Although I shall not attempt a lengthy or elaborate explication of "The Man with the Blue Guitar," a brief summary of the poem may help to show the changes in Stevens' poetry from the vivid poems celebrating external phenomena which he had published fourteen years earlier.

Section I is a dramatic posing of the problem of the artist in modern society. The people demand, paradoxically, that he play "a tune beyond us," and yet the tune must be "Of things exactly as they are" (CP, p. 165). In other words, the poet must create a myth for our time, "beyond us" in that its figures will be larger than life, and yet the myth must be true to the essential nature of "things exactly as they are." + quote

In a sense, section I is a definition of the term "myth," for the mythic hero is always "beyond us," yet the myth itself must be true to the deepest nature of the human psyche.

Section II drops the dialog form to become, not the exchange between artist and mass, but rather a musing dialectic within the mind of the shearsman. Sections III and IV are very important in the over-all context of Stevens' work, for they introduce the concept of "Man number one," the idea of the mythic abstract form of man to replace the idea of God. "The Man with the Blue Guitar" initiates Stevens' poetic ideal—to capture all human life on "one string," in one abstract hero who could summarize all of us. The difference between the defensive contentiousness of "Owl's Clover" and the bold affirmation of "Blue Guitar" is nowhere clearer than it is in section V. The masses have just summarized the conditions of their lives:

There are no shadows in our sun,

Day is desire and night is sleep.
There are no shadows anywhere.

The earth, for us, is flat and bare.
There are no shadows.
(CP, p. 167)

As if with the same voice, the poem offers a cure for a shadowless world.

Poetry

Exceeding music must take the place
Of empty heaven and its hymns,

Ourselves in poetry must take their place
Even in the chattering of your guitar.
(CP, p. 167)

The Man with the Blue Guitar   55

Disease and cure, "they" and "I," society and poet, are all elements of the poet's meditations, and out of the meditations comes the assertion that poetry can provide a "supreme fiction," a fiction which can replace the moribund mythology represented by "empty heaven."

Section VII begins with a phrase that might have been torn from *Harmonium:* "It is the sun that shares our works." Almost immediately, however, there is an encroachment upon that sunlight by the chill tones of *Ideas of Order*.

> The sun no longer shares our works
> And the earth is alive with creeping men,
>
> Mechanical beetles never quite warm . . .
>
> (CP, p. 168)

The motifs of coldness, alienation, and mechanism are familiar patterns in modern life, and Stevens had used them earlier. However, section VIII affirms the possibility of the blue guitar as ordering principle in the chaotic storm of reality. The artist can "Bring the storm to bear," and this is in itself a good. Section X shows the poet confronting the mythic too-human god who must be replaced by "Man number one." Stevens describes the mythic divinity as "him whom none believes,/ Whom all believe that all believe" (CP, p. 170). The scene is dramatic; the confrontation of poet and "pagan in a varnished car" is presented as a kind of one-act play, but the action, setting, and characters are all highly impressionistic. The action is truncated, the figures dreamlike, the setting fantastic and abstract. There is fine comic irony in the diminution of the anthropomorphic deity who will, after all, be topped by a "hoo-er" of "the slick trombones." Perhaps not even Goliath met so ignoble a defeat. Section XV presents another picture of modern life. Here is the ultimate alienation from the self—the gap between the present moment and our knowledge of it.

Am I a man that is dead

At a table on which the food is cold?
Is my thought a memory, not alive?

Is the spot on the floor, there, wine or blood
And whichever it may be, is it mine?
                    (CP, p. 173)

Such a questioning of the epistemology of experience and,
more important, the recognition that all thought may be a
form of memory is new to the poetry of Wallace Stevens.
This section contains the knowledge, never to be forgotten
by Stevens, that all human experience is forever cut off
from one who experiences because all of our senses give us
information at some distance in time and intensity from
the event. This meditation is on the nature and limitations
of the relationship between physical phenomena—the spot
on the floor, the food—and the mind of man.

Section XXI describes further the nature of "Man number
one." He must be

A substitute for all the gods:
This self, not that gold self aloft, . . .

Without shadows, without magnificence,
The flesh, the bone, the dirt, the stone.
                    (CP, p. 176)

Sections XXII and XXIII begin the task of reconciling the
opposing forces of the imagination and physical phenomena.

Poetry is the subject of the poem,
From this the poem issues and

To this returns. Between the two,
Between issue and return, there is

An absence in reality,
Things as they are. Or so we say.

The Man with the Blue Guitar   57

But are these separate? Is it
An absence for the poem, which acquires

Its true appearances there, sun's green,
Cloud's red, earth feeling, sky that thinks?

From these it takes. Perhaps it gives,
In the universal intercourse.

(CP, pp.176–77)

Since, for Stevens, "Poetry is the statement of the relation
between a man and his world" (OP, p. 172), section XII
illustrates his adage that "The theory of poetry is the theory
of life" (OP, p. 178). Our sense of existence is the product
of a "universal intercourse" between the mind and the
affluent earth, an intercourse in which the mind takes inspiration from sun, clouds, earth, and sky and in return provides them with exotic colors and with imagined emotions
and thoughts. And, having affirmed, however tentatively,
this balance between mind and soil, Stevens is left with
only "A few final solutions."

The reconciliation of the opposing forces of mind and
world is the subject of the first "final solution," that posed in
section XXIII. Stevens imagines a duet sung by

a voice in the clouds,

Another on earth, the one a voice
Of ether, the other smelling of drink.

(CP, p. 177)

The voice of ether prevails, and the result of the duet is that

all
Confusion [is] solved, as in a refrain

One keeps on playing year by year,
Concerning the nature of things as they are.

(CP, p. 177)

The dramatized exchange is obviously between figures circumscribed by the poet's mind, for the two voices are disem-

bodied and even wordless. They serve only as symbols for *concordia discors*, harmoniously reconciled opposites. From this point on, the changes in mood, intensity of impression, and figures who appear are rapid and continuous; perhaps in evolving his new concept of poetry Stevens wished to emphasize the constant motion that marks the interplay of world and imagination. At any rate, the figure for the poem shifts from that of a duet sung by disparate voices to that of a missal found in mud to that of a world balanced dexterously on the nose of a creator-clown. In the latter figure, verbs of motion abound. The world is "twirled," and as it spins,

> liquid cats
> Moved in the grass without a sound.

> They did not know that the grass went round.
> The cats had cats and the grass turned gray

> And the world had worlds, ai, this-a-way:
> The grass turned green and the grass turned gray. . . .
> (CP, p. 178)

The created world is a world of constant procreation and flowing change. Only the nose, the creative force which sets the world in motion, seems eternal and at rest.

Sections XXVI and XXVII both emphasize the same flux. In XXVI, while the imagination speeds to the world and returns, the poet tells us that "A mountainous music always seemed/ To be falling and to be passing away" (CP, p. 179). In XXVII the poet is "The demon that cannot be himself,/ That tours to shift the shifting scene" (CP, p. 180).

Stevens brings his evolved man-hero at last to Oxidia, the "Banal suburb" which might well have been the setting for most of *Ideas of Order*. In Oxidia, as in Jersey City, religious symbols have been subverted to utilitarian ends. The crosses in Oxidia are telephone poles and the leaping flames of holy fire come from "crusty stacks above machines." But when Oxidia is viewed by the hero-poet,

> Ecce, Oxidia is the seed
> Dropped out of this amber-ember pod,
>
> Oxidia is the soot of fire,
> Oxidia is Olympia.
>
> (CP, p. 182)

By living in the world, the poet is enabled to live beyond it. The foundry fires become purified, and the imagination sanctifies everyday reality and lifts it to the level of living myth. As section XXXI puts it, "Morning is not sun,/ It is this posture of the nerves" (CP, p. 182). All experience, and morning is experience, is more than external conditions, such phenomena as the sun represents. Experience is also a product of the nerves, of the internal alterations which we make in what we see.

The final stanza affirms creative man's freedom even in the surroundings of the twentieth century. How can we live in a world without the myth of Heaven and with no earthly Utopia in sight? Stevens says we can accept the earth and our lot in it if we recognize the power of the poetic imagination to transform and illuminate the world.

> The bread
> Will be our bread, the stone will be
>
> Our bed and we shall sleep by night.
> We shall forget by day, except
>
> The moments when we choose to play
> The imagined pine, the imagined jay.
>
> (CP, p. 184)

We can choose to live in the world, and the poet's blue guitar gives us the power to create ourselves and in that creation to create in turn the world in which we exist.

A companion poem of "The Man with the Blue Guitar," "A Thought Revolved," presents three possible ways of human life. The poem has four sections: *"The Mechanical Optimist," "Mystic Garden and Middling Beast," "Romanesque Affabulation,"* and *"The Leader."* The first and last of these show, respectively, the mechanical, unexamined life lived by the average citizen of Oxidia and life lived completely by reason, detached from emotion and from the pathos of reality. The central sections, appropriately enough, deal with central man, the poet and his affabulations.

The lady dying of diabetes in the first section is comforted by the myth of the afterlife, by "familiar things in a cheerful voice./ Like the night before Christmas and all the carols" (CP, p. 185). Her optimism, like the other aspects of her life, is "mechanical," Stevens' term of disapprobation for the unexamined, common life of twentieth-century man. Her values are utilitarian and vulgar, her myths comfortable and familiar, but without vitality.

The moralist hidalgo of the final section is, like Adam, alienated by too much knowledge from the world which was made for him.

> In how severe a book he read,
> Until his nose grew thin and taut
> And knowledge dropped upon his heart
> Its pitting poison, half the night.
> (CP, p. 186)

If the mechanical optimist was one who lived the unexamined life, the moralist hidalgo is the examiner of the unlived life. He is motionless, and appropriately so, for, as always in Stevens, life is motion, and the moralist is an enemy to life. He prefers "that gold self aloft" to the beggars who surround him in the streets, and by cutting himself off from reality he becomes "The central flaw in the solar morn" (CP, p. 187).

In contrast, Stevens' figure of the poet is very much of the "real" world; indeed, like Stevens himself, he is at home "among the cigar stores,/ Ryan's lunch, hatters, insurance

and medicines" (CP, p. 185). Although his world is fundamentally the same as that of the mechanical optimist, the
poet recognizes the value of "abstraction." Only to the fatu-
ous, the poet insists, is abstraction a vice, and in this statement we see what is wrong with the moralist hidalgo in
whom abstraction has become a flaw. The poet returns to
the idea of man which was introduced in "The Man with the
Blue Guitar." The remainder of section II presents a secular
genesis of the "outer captain, the inner saint" who is Stevens' "Romanesque Affabulation." The imagery associated
with major man suggests that he is composed of reconciled
opposites, that he resolves all contradictions and contains
all mysteries.

> The pine, the pillar and the priest
> The voice, the book, the hidden well,
> The faster's feast and heavy-fruited star,
> The father, the beater of the rigid drums,
>
> He that at midnight touches the guitar,
> The solitude, the barrier, the Pole
> In Paris, celui qui chante et pleure,
> Winter devising summer in its breast . . .
>
> (CP, p. 186)

Pine, pillar, and priest are all masculine figures, while
voice, book, and hidden well may be thought of as feminine.
The entire stanza suggests both rite and ritual; all of the
symbols used to describe the "outer captain, inner saint"
represent, or once represented, religious mysteries, and the
four lines are a wonderfully compressed history of man's
long engagement with the supernatural forces of his mysterious universe. He is also creator, player of the guitar; an
alien in his world, a Pole in Paris; one capable of immense
joy and immense grief, *celui qui chante et pleure;* and he is
one who constantly changes and develops, as winter de-
vises summer in its breast. The "earthly leader" must contain all heaven and all hell within himself, for intensity of

life must take the place of the mythology of afterlife. The idea of man, Stevens' affabulation, is of a race "that sings and weeps and knows not why." Unlike the moralist hidalgo, Stevens' heroic man lives so intensely that he attains "ignorance" in the very special way that Stevens uses the term. ("It may be that the ignorant man, alone,/ Has any chance to mate his life with life . . .) He represents the impossible ideal of unfallen man, a kind of Adamic figure who lives a life of pure, unmediated, and blissfully unselfconscious experience. He is one of the race which Stevens envisioned in *Harmonium*, the race of men who chant their boisterous devotion to the sun in "Sunday Morning," a race which can never exist except in the poetic imagination, for "The adventurer/ In humanity has not conceived of a race/ Completely physical in a physical world" (CP, p. 325).

The Man with the Blue Guitar succeeds in introducing a myth of man to replace the myth of God. The creation of a myth is, of necessity, a work of the imagination, an internal process of the mind. Therefore, *Blue Guitar* represents a turning inward in Wallace Stevens' search for a subject for poetry. The poet of *Harmonium* had been a destroyer of tarnished myths, and the poetry he produced had celebrated the glories of the phenomenal world. However, the Stevens who has experienced the disorders of *Ideas of Order* has learned that man must have a myth, a fiction, an ordering principle, if he is to endure. Without such a fiction, man finds the earth shadowless, barren, and cold; in such a world human life is a mechanical process in which the machines inexorably wear themselves out. *The Man with the Blue Guitar* is Stevens' poetic affirmation that, despite the fact that he is a native of Oxidia, "things are as I think they are/ And say they are on the blue guitar" (CP, p. 180).

Parts of a World

Frank Kermode has said of *Parts of a World* that "This book is nobody's favorite, though it contains many poems of very high quality. It is a book in which the poems do little to quicken each other, and the worst way to approach it is to try and [*sic*] read it through." [1] While it is true that, in any comparison among Stevens' volumes of poetry, *Parts of a World* is unlikely to be a favorite, I believe the book to be much more closely unified than Kermode suggests, and feel that precisely the proper way to approach the collection of poems is that way which Kermode sees to be "worst." That is, to be properly appreciated, *Parts of a World* should be "read through" with the assumption that Stevens intends the "parts" to make up a "world" when assembled in a volume.

The volume is transitional in many ways. It is a pivotal volume in the *Collected Poems*, for it is the fourth of seven volumes. It stands midway between the world of *Harmonium* and the world of *The Rock*, and there is much in the volume that reaches back to *Harmonium* and much that stretches forward toward *The Rock*. Stylistically, the collection is varied. In form and technique it straddles, some-

[1] Kermode, *Wallace Stevens*, p. 71.

times uncomfortably, the dramatic, externally oriented poetry of *Harmonium* and the quieter musings of the later meditative volumes.

Riddel underscores the transitional nature of the volume, and adds that "*Parts of a World* seemed upon appearance not only to move further toward abstraction, but to confirm a considerable loss of power." [2] It is odd to regard *Parts of a World* as moving "further toward abstraction," for not since *Harmonium* has Stevens created so many dramatic personas and placed them in such dramatic stage settings. Through the pages of *Parts of a World* move a multitude of splendidly dissimilar figures: Fat Jocundus, Master Soleil, Mrs. Alfred Uruguay, Lady Lowzen, the latest freed man, the man on the dump, the rabbit-king of the ghosts, the possessor of a weak mind in some unidentified mountains, the girl in the nightgown, the connoisseur of chaos, the anti-master-man, and the well-dressed man with a beard. Certainly *Parts of a World* with its dramatic monologues and its concrete situations and characters is the most dramatic collection of poems, *Harmonium* aside, in the work of Wallace Stevens.

I should like to suggest that *Parts of a World* is intended to be a kind of microcosm, a compressed world of progressive experiences which Stevens had undergone until 1942 and which at the same time serves as a point of departure for later work, notably "Notes toward a Supreme Fiction." The parts of the volume which go to make up the wholeness of Stevens' poetic symbol for the world are carefully ordered. In their arrangement, Stevens repeats the process of the internalization of experience, for the volume begins with concrete and dramatic poetry and moves inexorably to the longer poems of abstract discussion with which *Parts of a World* concludes. Moreover, the volume begins with individual men in various dramatic situations and ends with

[2] Riddel, *Clairvoyant Eye*, p. 150.

major man, the synthesis of individuals and the product of the imagination. The latest freed man must precede major man, for only in human freedom can the ultimate, vital abstraction be created.

The first twelve poems of *Parts of a World* were originally published as a unit entitled "Canonica" in *The Southern Review* (Autumn, 1938). All twelve are concerned with the problem of perception, the relationship of man and world. "Canonica" makes frequent use of the dramatic mode, and such figures as Fat Jocundus, the two workers of "Idiom of the Hero," the man on the dump, the speakers of "On the Road Home," and the latest freed man move, declaim, and act in the face of varied situations of conflict.

The dramatic figures of the early poems of *Parts of a World* are not concerned with the problems of perception which were treated in *Harmonium*. The question of whether man is the intelligence of his soil or the soil man's intelligence is wisely dropped, for its limited possibilities as a subject for poetry have already been explored. Instead, the dramatic personas of "Canonica" became vehicles for expressing the discontent Stevens feels for "our climate," the ideas, presuppositions, and myths which make up the "old descriptions of the world." Before a new mythos can be formed, the old must be swept away, and the early poems of *Parts of a World* attempt to do the sweeping. By scrapping the old images and the old truth, Stevens offers a world view that is considerably less permanent and less orderly than was the traditional view of the universe; Stevens' view emphasizes with a vengeance the idea that life is motion, for the world is seen to be a process rather than a finished product, an ever-changing creation rather than a completed still life.

Thus, as Stevens presents his dramatic figures in the process of apprehending a world freed of old ideas which distort perception, he suggests that the act of apprehension is in itself a form of creative activity rather than a form of passive reception. In a sense, this suggestion reverses the apparent decision of *Harmonium,* the idea that the world transforms the imagination. The imagination creates the world we perceive, and since the mind is never resting, never satisfied, it follows inevitably that the world is a continuing process of transformations, that all hope of static perfection is lost, and that our paradise must be imperfect if it is to be at all. By taking the position that we are the creators of our world, Stevens becomes dedicated to the romantic world view of an organic, ever-changing, imperfect universe.

In his "Prelude to Objects" Stevens charges the poet with the responsibility of being the creator of our world.

> conceive for the courts
> Of these academies, the diviner health
> Disclosed in common forms. Set up
> The rugged black, the image . . . .
> Take the place
> Of parents, lewdest of ancestors.
> We are conceived in your conceits.
>
> (CP, p. 195)

The "objects" to which this charge is a "prelude" are two pears, the subject of careful study in the next poem of *Parts of a World.* The observer makes every effort to study the pears objectively, scientifically, without evasion from "reality" by metaphor.

> Opusculum paedagogum.
> The pears are not viols,
> Nudes or bottles.
> They resemble nothing else.
>
> (CP, p. 196)

There is, of course, humor in this dry, scholarly beginning. In asserting that the pears are *not* "viols,/ Nudes or bottles" Stevens reminds us that indeed pears do resemble all of these things. The narrator finds himself in the position of the man who is told not to think about an elephant. The very attempt to fix a center, to will the world to remain static, is self-defeating. The center will not hold.

> The shadows of the pears
> Are blobs on the green cloth.
> The pears are not seen
> As the observer wills.
>
> (CP, p. 197)

In this final stanza the observer's attention has wandered beyond the pears to the shape of their shadows and the color of the tablecloth. The fruit suddenly takes on a context, enters into a new relationship, and the careful descriptions that have gone before are rendered inadequate. Shadows in Stevens usually represent products of the imagination; there are, for example, no shadows in the light which an electric lamp throws on a page of Euclid, as Stevens notes in "The Common Life." In "Study of Two Pears," the shadows cast by the pears prove too much. The seeker of untinted reality concedes defeat, and the resemblances rush in upon him.

The next poem in the volume, "The Glass of Water," is. another treatment of the same theme. In fact, it can be argued that "Prelude to Objects" and "The Glass of Water" clarify and augment the "minor work" which "The Study of Two Pears" represents. It would, perhaps, be possible to interpret "The Study of Two Pears" in many different ways had Stevens not carefully placed it in its present context in his *Collected Poems*. This tendency in Stevens to explain or enhance one poem by its juxtaposition with other poems is the best argument against the position of Kermode which advises against reading the volume of poems through and which asserts that "the poems do little to quicken each other."

The constantly changing nature of reality is carefully developed in "The Glass of Water," a poem which chooses a deliberately prosaic, stable object, a still life not unlike the two pears, to indicate that reality is a flowing series of endless confrontations of mind and physical universe. Stevens begins by showing that even the physical universe, the collocations of molecules and atoms, is unstable.

> That the glass would melt in heat,
> That the water would freeze in cold,
> Shows that this object is merely a state,
> One of many, between two poles.
>
> (CP, p. 197)

Stevens then directly compares the physical and the metaphysical.

In the metaphysical, there are these poles. Just as the water and the glass in the first stanza represent one state along a locus of possible physical points, the second stanza presents one of the millions of possible metaphors that the glass of water will support.

> Here in the centre stands the glass. Light
> Is the lion that comes down to drink. There
> And in that state, the glass is a pool.
> Ruddy are his eyes and ruddy are his claws
> When light comes down to wet his frothy jaws
>
> And in the water winding weeds move round.
>
> (CP, p. 197)

Given the light, the resemblances that Stevens views as the basis for all poetry begin. The light is like a lion, perhaps in its "ruddy" color, perhaps in the fact that it comes down to the water like a beast coming to drink. Given that resemblance, the relationship of light to glass becomes that of lion to pool. The phrase "in that state" reminds the reader that the glass becomes a pool only while the light is transformed by the imagination into a lion. There is a suggestion of endless other states to be explored, for

> there and in another state—the refractions,
> The *metaphysica,* the plastic parts of poems
> Crash in the mind . . .
>
> (CP, p. 197)

But Stevens will not follow these possibilities as he does in other poems—for example, "Thirteen Ways of Looking at a Blackbird" or "Sea Surface Full of Clouds." His purpose in "The Glass of Water" is not to present thirteen ways of looking at a glass of water, but rather to make a statement about the changing nature of reality. The glass of water is used as an illustration of an abstract thesis, while the blackbird of the "Thirteen Ways" is in itself the subject of its poem.

Riddel asserts that "fat Jocundus" is a figure for the poet, and as such he "is a seeker after the centre, not the surface, the changeless, not the flowing waters." [3] I find this identification of the poet and Jocundus dubious, for the poet is precisely the man who most realizes that there is no center, but that there are only "states," and that life is a process of continuous discovery. In his worrying about what stands in the center, the jocund Jocundus seems very like the "mechanical optimist" of "A Thought Revolved." To Jocundus a glass of water is only something to be drunk, but it is not he whose voice concludes the poem.

It is a state, this spring among the politicians
Playing cards. In a village of the idigenes,
One would still have to discover. Among the dogs and dung,
One would continue to contend with one's ideas.
(CP, p. 198)

The voice is that of the poet-narrator, raised in answer to Jocundus, seeker after certainty, a center. Stevens suggests that even in a society in which life is reduced to its barest essentials, the mind will continue to be dissatisfied and to discover. The dogs and dung of the indigenes and the politicians of twentieth-century America, like the glass of water, exist as possible states, "One of many, between two poles." Reality is not fixed, but fluid, not a vital center, but a locus of possible points which will satisfy the conditions of a relationship between the world and the mind.

[3] Ibid., p. 155.

Having asserted the creative possibilities of perception, Stevens turns to the problem of freeing the imagination from various centers that have been postulated as the truth and which are inimical to poetry, and hence to life. In "Idiom of the Hero," Stevens rejects the Marxian truth of the Utopia predicted as an article of faith by two workers. "I heard two workers say, 'This chaos/ Will soon be ended'" (CP, p. 200). Stevens rejects this assertion as illusion, accepting chaos as part of the human condition. Imperfection is our lot, and the poet is therefore

> the poorest of all.
> I know that I cannot be mended,
>
> Out of the clouds, pomp of the air,
> By which at least I am befriended.
>> (CP, p. 201)

The same idea is expressed in "On the Road Home," a dialog in which the narrator learns that when one rejects "the truth," a unifying principle such as Marxism or Christianity, that he is befriended by the "good air" of what remains. The beauty of earth is perceived fully only by the man who does not seek to go beyond the earth, who does not insist on perfection in the midst of our imperfection.

> It was when I said,
> "There is no such thing as the truth,"
> That the grapes seemed fatter.
> The fox ran out of his hole. . . .
>
> It was at that time, that the silence was largest
> And longest, the night was roundest,
> The fragrance of the autumn warmest,
> Closest and strongest.
>> (CP, pp. 203–204)

There is a transformation here, an awakening from the images in "The Man on the Dump," and an escape from the truth, as in "The Latest Freed Man."

One image pattern that permeates *Parts of a World* is the

pattern of awakening, of throwing off the grogginess of custom and tradition and prejudgment. The latest freed man, the narrator of "On the Road Home," the man on the dump, and the poet who overhears the workers all affirm the same need to cast off the "old descriptions of the world" and to see the landscape "like a man without a doctrine."

The most pernicious of the old descriptions, the notion that the earth is made for man by a "too human god," that we are "sponsored" on this planet, and that it is "our own" is satirized in "A Rabbit as King of the Ghosts." The rabbit, close cousin to Chaucer's Chantecler, is a victim of hubris, the victim of the misconception that

> the light is a rabbit-light,
> In which everything is meant for you
> And nothing need be explained . . .
>
> (CP, p. 209)

In Stevens' imagery from the very beginning, ghosts are associated with fantasy, and, from the firecat of "Earthy Anecdote" on, cats are identified with reality, including the ultimate reality, death. Thus, as one reads "A Rabbit as King of the Ghosts," it is impossible to forget the nature of cats and rabbits, and one senses impending doom in the rabbit's conception of "a self that fills the four corners of night," while the "red cat hides away in the fur-light." The poem is a parable, illustrating in comic form the tragedy of forgetting the lesson to be offered by "Notes toward a Supreme Fiction":

> we live in a place
> That is not our own and, much more, not ourselves
> And hard it is in spite of blazoned days.
>
> (CP, p. 383)

The image of "sleepers," used to represent the mass of men who do not live intensively, is one which Stevens might well have borrowed from Thoreau, who remarked that the millions are awake enough for physical labor; but only one in a million is awake enough for effective intellectual exertion, only one in a hunderd million to a poetic or divine life. To be awake is to be alive. I have never yet met a man who was quite awake. How could I have looked him in the face?

(*Walden*, "Where I Lived, and What I Lived For")

The narrator of "A Weak Mind in the Mountains" recognizes the possibilities of the human mind, realizes what could have been had his mind been strong enough to withstand the chaos of the wind of Iceland and the wind of Ceylon, the north and south winds.

> Yet there was a man within me
> Could have risen to the clouds,
> Could have touched these winds,
> Bent and broken them down,
> Could have stood up sharply in the sky.
>
> (CP, p. 212)

The heights which the narrator might have reached, reminiscent of the height of Stevens' major man, suggest that he might have been that man who, having had time to think enough, might have brought order out of the chaos of reality. The winds could have been "broken down." However, the mind is "weak," and

> The black wind of the sea
> And the green wind
> Whirled upon me.
> The blood of the mind fell
> To the floor. I slept.

The tension of the poem is, of course, between human potential and human actuality, between the shaping powers of the mind which "Could have risen to the clouds" and the flatness of "I slept."

Another sleeper, but one who is on the verge of becoming "free" and "awake" is the girl in the nightgown. The girl is prudent, for the lights in her room go out before the shades go up. From her window she looks out into a night which Stevens endows with several images of transformation. Winter is ending and the waking of the earth coincides with the girl's awakening. The winter is

> Like a tottering, a falling and an end,
> Again and again, always there, . . .
>
> A revolution of things colliding.
>
> (CP, p. 214)

The girl, apparently on the verge of puberty, senses a change in the nature of the night, a change which is the reflection of her own growth.

> Once it was, the repose of night,
> Was a place, strong place, in which to sleep.
> It is shaken now. It will burst into flames,
> Either now or tomorrow or the day after that.
>
> (CP, p. 214)

The flames would seem to signify intensity, passion of some sort, and the girl would seem to give promise of never becoming one of the women of "The Common Life" who have "only one side."

Another of the transformed, freed figures in *Parts of a World* is the hero of "Contrary Theses (II)." Once again, the setting is a season of transition, this time, autumn. The hero walks, seeking refuge from the "bombastic intimations of winter/ And the martyrs a la mode." As he walks, still drugged by intimations of winter, the imagery associated with his surroundings is mechanical and lifeless.

> One chemical afternoon in mid-autumn,
> When the grand mechanics of earth and sky were near,
> Even the leaves of the locust were yellow then,
>
> He walked with his year-old boy on his shoulder.
> The sun shone and the dog barked and the baby slept.
>
> (CP, p. 270)

The afternoon is "chemical," and the view of the earth is mechanical. The "parts" of the world are just that, "parts," unrelated except accidentally. The dog barks and the sun shines and the baby sleeps, but the actions are separate, not parts of an abstract whole in which they are but "contours."

Suddenly the imagery changes. "The leaves were falling like notes from a piano." With the metaphor of leaves like parts of a harmonious whole, a composition, the hero has a momentary vision. "The abstract was suddenly there and gone again. . . . The abstract that he saw, like the locust leaves, plainly." The transience of the moment of transcendence leaves one with a feeling not unlike that which arises from Keats's great odes. Unity has been glimpsed, and life will never again be quite the same, but we return nonetheless to the same "common life," the mechanical world of "the weariness, the fever, and the fret."

The point that only the man of imagination can "mate his life with life" can be made negatively as well as positively. *Parts of World* contains a group of poems depicting the unlived life of the sleepers, and the poems of transformation are juxtaposed with them effectively. Such poems as "Loneliness in Jersey City," "Anything Is Beautiful if You Say It Is," "Forces, the Will & the Weather," and "The Common Life" are all designed to point to the shallowness of modern life. Modern man lives "Without ideas in a land without ideas" (CP, p. 228); he dwells in "a morbid light" in which "a man is a result,/ A demonstration . . ." (CP, p. 221). A more impressionistic treatment of the sleepers motif occurs in "On the Adequacy of Landscape." The inhabitants of the landscape are empty for the most part, although there are exceptions, people who, like the latest freed man, are "sensible to pain" and who awaken "clawing at their beds/ To be again" (CP, p. 244). The majority shrink to "an insensible,/ Small oblivion," afraid of both the "blood-red redness of the sun" of the external world and of the "bright, discursive wings" of the little owl which might represent the "central things" that only the imagination can produce. Thus, to draw back from both red bird and owl is to admit fear of the powers of the mind as well as fear of the pain of sensory experience.

The obvious companion piece to "On the Adequacy of Landscape" is its immediate predecessor in *The Collected Poems,* "Landscape with Boat." The first line of the poem presents the cast—"An anti-master-man, floribund ascetic" (CP, p. 241). The anti-master-man is the one who, unlike the man who lives the common life, has rejected the moribund mythologies of haunted heaven and has decided to live without any imaginative distortion at all. Like fat Jocundus, the anti-master-man seeks an absolute reality, a center which will be "neutral," that is, an objective "truth beyond all truths." Like the narrator of "On the Road Home," the anti-master-man must learn that "there is no such thing as the truth," and, having accepted that proposition, he will realize "the adequacy of landscape," for the grapes will then seem fatter.

The poem begins with the anti-master-man's action of doing away with imaginative colorings

> He brushed away the thunder, then the clouds,
> Then the colossal illusion of heaven. Yet still
> The sky was blue. He wanted imperceptible air.
> He wanted to see. He wanted the eye to see
> And not be touched by blue. . . .
> (CP, p. 241)

But, despite his brushings, the sky remains the blue shade of the imagination; the eye is still touched by blue. Enck has described such a man as one "whose outlook works against the mastery of the intricacy of reality," [4] and this is so, for the denial of the mind's part in creating reality oversimplifies the complex, ever-shifting relationship which human beings experience and call "reality." A scientist

[4] Enck, *Wallace Stevens,* p. 144.

might make such a mistake, but Stevens never would. Riddel puts it differently, but his point is the same. He asserts that out of the anti-master-man's struggle to find a neutral center, the anti-master-man will at last "discover the identity of self, which *is* because it is necessary that there be a mind before the world of parts has any quality, any life." [5] Only the self, the mind, can create a unity or abstraction out of the disparate parts of our landscape. But the anti-master-man

> never supposed
> That he might be truth, himself, or part of it,
> That the things that he rejected might be part
> And the irregular turquoise, part, the perceptible blue
> Grown denser, part, the eye so touched, so played
> Upon by clouds, the ear so magnified
> By thunder, parts, and all these things together,
> Parts, and more things, parts. . . .
>   (CP, p. 242)

It is the human mind which perceives an abstract of which the parts of the world are "contours." As in "Contrary Theses (II)," in which the walker discovers "The premiss [*sic*] from which all things were conclusions" (CP, p. 270), the anti-master-man might discover, "Had he been better able to suppose," in the landscape about him that "The thing I hum appears to be/ The rhythm of this celestial pantomime" (CP, p. 243).

The conflict of opposed values, the search for a reality untouched by falsifying blue, and the search for an abstract, imagined land is dramatized in "Mrs. Alfred Uruguay," a poem in which the conflicting values are represented by dramatic personas. Like the anti-master man, Mrs. Uruguay is an ascetic, one who says no to everything to get at "the real."

[5] Riddel, *Clairvoyant Eye*, p. 157.

And for her,
To be, regardless of velvet, could never be more
Than to be, she could never differently be,
Her no and no made yes impossible.

(CP, p. 249)

By denying the transformations which moonlight works
upon the world, Mrs. Uruguay rides forever *toward* the real,
but there is no suggestion that she will arrive there. Instead,
the works of moonlight crumble to "degenerate forms," and
even her mule "wished for a bell,/ Wished faithfully for a
falsifying bell."

Suddenly a rider "on a horse all will" passes her going in
the opposite direction.

Who was it passed her there on a horse all will,
What figure of capable imagination?
Whose horse clattered on the road on which she rose,
As it descended, blind to her velvet and
The moonlight? Was it a rider intent on the sun,
A youth, a lover with phosphorescent hair,
Dressed poorly, arrogant of his streaming forces,
Lost in an integration of the martyrs' bones,
Rushing from what was real; and capable?

(CP, p. 249)

The figure is the poet-hero, and much can be learned from
studying the trappings with which Stevens invests him. The
horse which bears him is "all will," an appropriate motivat-
ing force for the poet. It is the mind's will, never satisfied
and constantly moving, which produces the "supreme fiction." The horse of the "figure of capable imagination" is a
symbolic representation of the mind's will to create "the
imagined land." The "capable" imagination must be distin-
guished from the imagination which produces "degenerate
forms," images for the dump. The rider, being capable,
takes no interest in the velvet of Mrs. Uruguay nor the
moonlight of crumbled forms through which she rides. In-

stead, he is intent on the sun, and his intensity indicates love of the physical universe; this is doubtless why Stevens characterizes him as a "lover." He is like those "people sensible to pain" in "On the Adequacy of Landscape" who

> turn toward the cocks
> And toward the start of day and trees
> And light behind the body of night
> And sun . . .
>   (CP, p. 244)

He rushes from the barren rock of reality toward which Mrs. Uruguay rides, and although the villages sleep as he rides, his very presence brings dreams. It is important that one not read the adjective "capable" in the last line of the stanza cited above as modifying "what was real." It refers, as it does earlier in the stanza, to the rider. The "real," that barren rock, is never capable by itself. It creates nothing, if, indeed, it exists at all except as a necessary postulate of the mind, a starting point from which the horse of will must dash. Mrs. Uruguay will discover that, journey as she will, "Yet still/ The sky [will be] blue." Her elegance "must struggle"; her velvet and moonlight are degenerate forms. The ultimate elegance is that which only the poet can create "in his mind": "the imagined land." However, like the barren rock of phenomenal, undistorted "reality," the ultimate "imagined land" can only be a creation which the mind postulates but never reaches. Although the imagined land may be created by the rider-poet, and although it "may suffice" briefly, the process of creation must be continuous; horse and rider must never cease and the meditation which the will engenders must be never-ending.

Stevens abandons the dramatic form in two short poems which appear almost to be preparations for the longer abstract poems which conclude *Parts of a World*. Both poems begin with abstract statements, and each is almost a definition of poetry. Combining them, we find that poetry is the action of the mind "to find what will suffice." In short, the poet must create an "imagined land" which will take the place of the "romantic tenements" in which we now live. Stevens realizes that the *Weltanschauung* of twentieth-century man must be created, for the old world views will no longer suffice. The world of the eighteenth century, even the world of the nineteenth century, was constricted by what those ages believed "was in the script." Man, the creation of a benevolent Creator, was essentially good, and human destiny was assured. By 1942, such an optimistic view had been trampled in the blood of the "war to end war" and the war that was then going on.

The poetic mind, in finding what would suffice as a world view for the twentieth century, had "to content the reason concerning war," had

> to persuade that war is part of itself,
> A manner of thinking, a mode
> Of destroying . . .
> (CP, p. 239)

Man must accept his own evil nature if he is to discover the good of which he is capable. The mind of the poet, "A man at the centre of man," contains "the fury of a race of men" as well as "the central good." Knowing its own capacity for destruction, the mind cannot tolerate the romantic tenements which falsify the human condition. Daniel Fuchs is correct when he says that "The word 'romantic' here . . . has the force of sentimental." Perhaps he is on less sure ground when he continues, "The title ['Man and Bottle"] seems to imply that this courageous assertion must be sustained by spirits at times, but earthly ones to be sure." [6] However, few critics have cared to tackle the problem of the relation of this title to its poem, and Fuch's suggestion would seem to win the field by default.

Perhaps the most significant element in "Man and Bottle"

[6] Fuchs, *The Comic Spirit of Wallace Stevens*, p. 89.

is the identification in its opening sentence of the mind, the poem and the central man. The growing importance of the figure of the "man at the centre of men" in Stevens' poetry, then, is also a growth in the importance of the mind and the poem. The mind and the act of the mind are joined and apotheosized as Stevens begins his journey toward summer, autumn, and the concluding rock.

The turning inward of Stevens' poetry in the later poems of *Parts of a World* is apparent in the setting which Stevens creates for "Of Modern Poetry." Whereas *Harmonium* was set, for the most part, in the external world, the more meditative form which Stevens begins to use more and more often requires a setting which can stand for the mind itself. There is never any question of our taking the "theater" in "Of Modern Poetry" to be literal, for its changes and its elusive vagueness make it far too impressionistic to be a part of objective reality. Frank Doggett is correct in seeing the changing theaters of the poem as representations of two kinds of mind, "the older mind that conceives of the world as a defined and given external and the modern mind that has a sense of the imagined world and must continually improvise 'what will suffice.'" [7] Stevens' poems are now poems of the mind and the mind's actions, but he still finds it necessary to objectify the mind as a symbol, although the theater is much too vaguely defined to function very well as a true symbol. The comparison of mind and theater is much more on the order of an analogy, a comparison offered to clarify a point, than the sort of symbolic representation one might find in other poets. Nonetheless, the objectifying of the mind as a theater does keep the poem from being purely philosophical or meditative. It is a poetic thesis, and the thesis is illustrated by the comparison of the mind with the two kinds of theater.

In "Of Modern Poetry" Stevens explains what is meant by

[7] Doggett, *Stevens' Poetry of Thought*, pp. 64–65.

"modern" as the term appears in the poetry. The mind, in finding what will suffice,

> has to be living, to learn the speech of the place.
> It has to face the men of the time and to meet
> The women of the time. It has to think about war . . .
> (CP, p. 240)

The mind does not find satisfaction in the set scene and pat script of the old theater, but finds it instead in actions which serve to get at the texture of life.

> It must
> Be the finding of a satisfaction, and may
> Be a man skating, a woman dancing, a woman
> Combing. The poem of the act of the mind.
> (CP, p. 240)

The three examples which Stevens selects from an indefinite number of possible examples are interesting, for they suggest the sort of things which Stevens seems to regard as *sufficient* experience. All are actions which, though having a beginning and an end, are fluid and continuous. Life *is* motion, a continuum in which each movement is a stimulus to new movement. Each of the actions of the skater, dancer, and comber flows smoothly out of the action of the moment before and into the action of the next moment. Thus, all one need do to get at the texture of the world is focus on such an action. The mind flows from image to image as the body of the skater flows over the ice, and the process itself is the finding of satisfaction. It is not the image or single poem that is produced which will ever suffice, but the action of the mind as the will impels it to make sounds "passing through sudden rightnesses," which in turn must give way to new rightnesses. The process of the mind in the act of finding what will suffice is such that first what will not suffice and what will no longer suffice must be destroyed. Next the mind must create a new stage, a new world view, and within the framework of a new mythology it must produce the actions and the sounds which, however momentarily, will "wholly [contain] the mind."

In a 1945 *Sewanee Review* article entitled "The Genre of Wallace Stevens," Hi Simons attempts to "define the genre of Stevens' poems" while answering two reviews of *Parts of a World.* Simons makes no distinction, or seems to make none, between the genre of *Harmonium* and the genre of *Parts of a World,* and in illustrating his view of Stevens' work he uses only "Asides on the Oboe," a poem from *Parts of a World,* which is quite different from such works as "On the Road Home" or "Girl in a Nightgown." Each of the latter two poems has a relatively dramatic framework, employs setting and characters, and does not give the effect of meditation so much as the effect of an event which meditation may invest with meaning. Nonetheless, Simons' view of Stevens' poetry is extremely useful in describing the kind of poetry to which Stevens turns at the end of *Parts of a World* and which he perfects in *Notes toward a Supreme Fiction.* In writing of Stevens' poetic form, Simons points out that Stevens is the creator of a genre "that was new in its time, . . . a type of poem that may be called a lyric of ideas, an intellectual lyric." Because "Asides on the Oboe" has been explicated so often, I shall not explicate it here. The interpretation which Simons offers is excellent, and I can do little more than recommend it. More to the purpose in this discussion is Simons' emphasis upon the "intellectual" nature of the poetry he is explicating. The genre of Wallace Stevens, Simons says, is defined in part by his *wit,* which is "of the same general nature as that of the Metaphysicals. . . . it is the factor of reasonableness underlying the lyric graces of his peculiarly characteristic poem of ideas." [8] The increased intellectual complexity of Stevens' poetry, his demand for an ever-greater mental engagement on the part of

[8] Simons, "The Genre of Wallace Stevens," p. 51.

his reader, represents the most marked development that takes place in *Parts of a World*.

With the opening lines of "Asides on the Oboe" Stevens turns his back forever on the possibility of once again going naked in Eden.

> The prologues are over. It is a question, now,
> Of final belief. So, say that the final belief
> Must be in a fiction. It is time to choose.
>
> (CP, p. 250)

The four meditative poems which conclude *Parts of a World*—"Asides on the Oboe," "Extracts from Addresses to the Academy of Fine Ideas," "Montrachet-le-Jardin," and "Examination of the Hero in a Time of War"—mark a significant change in Stevens' style, theme, and tone. The sense of the mind in process, creating as it watches itself create, the feeling of the intellectual nature of the poetic exercise, the sense of reasonableness underneath the music of the poem, are present in all four works. Joseph Riddel illuminates the important difference between these poems and Stevens' earlier work:

> Stevens' pursuit of an idea takes a severe toll in style, perhaps because he is making a significant transition from a poetry of perception to a poetry of the act of the mind. . . . he does not yet have full control of the metaphor which will blood an abstraction or draw out the thread of an idea into a feeling.[9]

The abstract idea of the "supreme fiction," a hero in a heroic land, is not "blooded," as Riddel puts it, in *Parts of a World*. The hero himself is not fully created. Instead, Stevens in these meditative poems turns the problem of creating such a fiction over and over in his mind; the effect is precisely that of a man thinking out loud. In this case, the thoughts are truly "meditations upon one string," and they

[9] Riddel, *Clairvoyant Eye*, p. 162.

are concerned less with the final fictitious abstraction than with the conditions which have convinced Stevens that "the final belief must be in a fiction."

Each includes, as one might expect, a regretful rejection of the possibility of the sufficiency of the physical universe alone. *Harmonium* and the Edenic dream are laid to rest. In "Asides on the Oboe" the sweetness of life is symbolized by jasmine, but the knowledge of death and human hatred "prevent the jasmine scent" in a time of war. "It was not," Stevens remarks sadly, "as if the jasmine ever returned" (CP, p. 251). In "Extracts," the speaker affirms the artificial nature of the world.

> Where is that summer warm enough to walk
> Among the lascivious poisons, clean of them,
> And in what covert may we, naked, be
> Beyond the knowledge of nakedness, as part
> Of reality, beyond the knowledge of what
> Is real, part of a land beyond the mind?
>
> (CP, p. 252)

The season does not exist, for man's knowledge prevents him from being "part of reality." Stevens may elsewhere reject "haunted heaven," but he is a believer in a secular and poetic kind of original sin, in man's alienation from his world through knowledge. "Montrachet-le-Jardin" begins with a reference to the past, a reference, perhaps to *Harmonium*.

> What more is there to love than I have loved?
> And if there be nothing more, O bright, O bright,
> The chick, the chidder-barn and grassy chives . . .
>
> Chome! clicks the clock, if there be nothing more.
>
> (CP, p. 260)

"Chome" indeed, for, as Stevens affirmed in *Ideas of Order,* the sensualist (the hedonist, if one will) finds "wormy metaphors" at the core of all his bright poems of earth.

A little while of Terra Paradise
I dreamed . . .

But in that dream a heavy difference
Kept waking and a mournful sense sought out,
In vain, life's season or death's element.
(CP, p. 263)

In order to save oneself from the hedonist's despair, one must have "something more to love," and that something must be "A shadow in the mind." The final love must be a fiction or there is only the ticking clock. "In a time of war" man finds that "Death is my/ Master and without light I dwell." The poems of our climate will be harsh indeed, a "click click" of machines and the roar of dynamite, and our belief will be in the "Got" of the machines of destruction. And out of this climate, because one can no longer believe in ecstatic communions with the weather, Stevens insists on belief in the hero, for "Unless we believe in the hero, what is there/ To believe?" (CP, p. 275).

All four of the poems deal with the existence of evil, not only with the evil of war, but with the evil that is inherent simply in our being what and where we are. Thus, from one point of view, all four poems are dissertations on how to cope with evil, the "evil" of the clicking clock as well as the evil of the clicking machinery of war. One must begin by rejecting those "obsolete fictions," all of the suggestions of immortality with which man has drugged himself. In "Asides on the Oboe" they are "That obsolete fiction of the wide river in/ An empty land; the gods that Boucher killed" (CP, p. 250). In "Extracts" they are "helpful things" said by "Helpful philosophers": "Plato, the reddened flower, the erotic bird" (CP, p. 253). "Plato" would seem to be a reference to that philosopher's discussion of the alternatives in death. The "reddened flower" suggests any one of a number of regenerated gods whose blood, according to legend, changed the colors of the flowers on which it fell. The "erotic bird" might be the Phoenix, symbol of rebirth, or it might refer to any of the migratory birds believed by primitive tribes to contain the power to make crops grow. In "Examination of the Hero in a Time of War" we learn that the people are sick "of each old romance returning,/ Of each old revolving dance . . ." (CP, p. 274).

These old ways of accounting for evil give way to a new one which embraces evil as part of the supreme fiction, as a necessary and harmonious part of the human abstract. "We found the sum of men. We found,/ If we found the central evil, the central good" (CP, p. 251). Yet, evil cannot be the ultimate state of this life, for Stevens insists that "Stanzas of final peace/ Lie in the heart's residuum."

> How can
> We chant if we live in evil and afterward
> Lie harshly buried there?
>
> If earth dissolves
> Its evil after death, it dissolves it while
> We live. Thence come the final chants . . .
> (CP, p. 259)

In "Montrachet-le-Jardin" the chant enables man to become the hero of his world. Buried in the "heart's residuum" like the collective knowledge which Jung ascribes to the human unconscious mind are "the earliest poems of the world/ In which man is the hero" (CP, p. 261). These poems serve as a talisman against evil, a way past "the x malisons of other men" and on to "the hero land" where "The poison in the blood will have been purged" (CP, p. 262). Evil is overcome when man elevates himself to the level of living myth, for to become one with the "tallest hero" is to gain a measure of immortality and to overcome the evil which has alienated us from our world and from ourselves.

Belief in the hero can save us in "a time of war," a time which, Riddel asserts, is for Stevens "a metaphor for modern reality." "The hero," Riddel says, "is the self, which alone can save itself, there being no other gods." [10] How the hero, man elevated to the level of myth, can save himself is implied in his attributes.

> We have and are the man, capable
> Of his brave quickenings, the human
> Accelerations that seem inhuman.
>> (CP, p. 279)

Or again the hero

> is the heroic
> Actor and act but not divided.
> It is a part of his conception,
> That he be not conceived, being real.
> Say that the hero is his nation,
> In him made one, and in that saying
> Destroy all references. This actor
> Is anonymous and cannot help it.
>> (CP, p. 279)

Stevens' man who "in a thousand diamonds sums us up" is man without the encumbering particulars of sex, age, and vocation, man as he might be without the limitations of living, as we must, in this time, in that place. He is representative of the total consciousness of the human race, a consciousness which can, of course, be only partial in the individual. The sustaining, timeless image of the central man and the classic, impersonal forms of his deeds are the materials out of which Stevens attempts to create a myth designed to shore up the ruins in which twentieth-century man is a tenant.

It is the poet's, the artist's, duty to enlarge man's vision, to make the individual embrace the "hero" and "meditate him over and over" until at last he arrives at the "man-man," the abstract image of the totality of humanity.

Is it a fiction, this abstract entity? It is, but Stevens ponders the nature of truth in the concluding stanza of

[10] Ibid., pp. 162–63.

"Examination of the Hero in a Time of War," the last words of *Parts of a World*.

> After the hero, the familiar
> Man makes the hero artificial.
> But was the summer false? The hero?
> How did we come to think that autumn
> Was the veritable season, that familiar
> Man was the veritable man? So
> Summer, jangling the savagest diamonds and
> Dressed in its azure-doubled crimsons,
> May truly bear its heroic fortunes
> For the large, the solitary figure.
>
> (CP, pp. 280–81)

Thus, Stevens, like Keats, asserts the truth of the beautiful in the face of the demands of ugly reality. Stevens would have appreciated Richard Harter Fogle's comment on Keats's "Ode on a Grecian Urn." "Is not the worse the true, the better the illusion. Should we not change the meaning of truth?" [11]

[11] Richard Harter Fogle, *PMLA*, Vol. LXVIII, No. 3 (1953), 218.

Transport to Summer

After the vacillations of the early pages of *Parts of a World*, after Stevens had chosen to follow the nameless rider to the imagined land rather than Mrs. Uruguay to her blank rock of undistorted "reality," after he decided that the final belief must be in fiction, Stevens turned to "Summer, jangling the savagest diamonds and/ Dressed in its azure-doubled crimsons" (CP, p. 281) as a poetic figuration for a fictive creation which might be worthy of the adjective "supreme." In turning from "true autumn" and "the familiar man," Stevens begins a poetic movement toward an acceptance of the fictive as the "veritable," an acceptance which is made with the full realization that what is chosen is not reality, but is in every way "artificial." The journey, or "transport," to summer is an act of faith, an acceptance of that which bears "heroic fortunes" as being somehow truer than is the commonplace view of man and his world which we ordinarily think of as representative of reality. *Parts of a World* raises the fundamental question of the nature of truth, a question which Stevens answers for better or for worse in "Examination of the Hero in a Time of War," a poem which chooses the hero over the familiar man, the oriole over the crow. It is appropriate that after examining the hero in time of war and finding him to be of solid stuff, we be transported to summer. The hero, or major man, is developed and discussed much further in *Transport to Summer* and is as sure a link between that volume and *Parts of a World* as were the voices of the monocled uncle and Don Joost between *Harmonium* and *Ideas of Order*.

It is by now a critical commonplace that by 1947 Stevens' verse form had become "suitable to expository writing" and that the poet had an interest in "generalized themes" which invited "over-extension and an element of vagueness." [1] However, as Frank Kermode has indicated, "This might be stated less pejoratively: Stevens had developed to an extraordinary degree a manner of commenting upon the text of reality and also upon the commentary which, he said, was equally a part of the real." [2] Even Kermode has failed to pay proper tribute to the magnificent courage of Stevens' leap of poetic faith. By insisting that the supreme fiction must be an act of the mind, and by turning increasingly inward to meditate among those highly personal figures of the imagination and phenomenal reality which had grown up over a lifetime of creative imaginings, Stevens risked his poetic reputation and his last productive years on the truth of his esthetic principles. If he is wrong, if the "supreme fiction" cannot be "abstract," even in the special sense in which he uses the term, his affirmation is nonetheless remarkable. Stevens must have known that the major work of *Transport to Summer*, a work which may well have been his most ambitious undertaking, would never be widely read. Its movements and configurations depend so heavily on the saturation of the reader in Stevens' poetic world that the poem can hardly be read in isolation. One usually is introduced to Stevens through the poems of *Harmonium*, poems which lose little from being set in the comparative isolation of anthologies. "Sunday Morning," "Peter Quince at the Clavier," and "The Emperor of Ice Cream" are among Ste-

---

[1] O'Connor, *The Shaping Spirit*, p. 131.
[2] Kermode, *Wallace Stevens*, p. 95.

vens' best-known poems, but none of them is so ambitious
an effort as is "Notes toward a Supreme Fiction" or as is
"Esthétique du Mal."

Transport to Summer is a volume of poetry of explicit
statement, or at least poetry in which the symbols are used
so regularly and so allegorically that they themselves become relatively abstract and differ but little from direct
statement. By the 1940's Stevens thinks in iambic pentameter, and the freedom with which he uses the form suggests
that rhythm and the processes of thought had become so
fused that poetry and thought were one. The commonplace
that Riddel seems to accept in *The Clairvoyant Eye,* that
"Stevens at this time had derived an idiom much less vital
to express a theme much more abstract" (p. 305), may be a
bit unfair. If it is true that Stevens turns more and more
inward for his poetic subjects, it is equally true that there is
little in *Harmonium* which compares favorably with section
XI or section XV, to choose the obvious examples of excellence, of "Esthétique du Mal." Stevens had not since the
final lines of "Sunday Morning" articulated the tragi-comic
nature of the human condition with the vitality of "Notes
toward a Supreme Fiction":

> From this the poem springs: that we live in a place
> That is not our own and, much more, not ourselves
> And hard it is in spite of blazoned days.
>
> (CP, p. 383)

At least, as Riddel admits, *Transport to Summer* "surprised
a great many critics who had predicted that the vigor, the
brio, of *Harmonium* had finally exhausted itself in the pat-
ent exercises of *Parts of a World*." [3]

Perhaps the most accurate summation of the worth of
Transport to Summer is that of Louis L. Martz, who describes the volume as being "meditative poetry that is in
every way the equal of his great, first volume of hedonist

---

[3] Riddel, *Clairvoyant Eye,* p. 222.

poetry. It is not a question of setting up divisions, but of watching recessive elements in the early poetry develop into dominance." [4] The elements which emerge in *Transport to Summer* as dominant would indeed seem to be familiar ones—the problem of how to cope with the evil in the human condition, the problem of perception, or the relationship of mind and world, and the problem of evolving a supreme fiction which had been most recessive in *Harmonium*, but which had become central by 1947. In fact, in *Transport to Summer*, having committed himself to the notion that the final belief must be in a fiction, Stevens found all other concerns secondary. Evil, for example, becomes significant because a supreme fiction which does not cope with its existence is false in a pejorative sense. The fiction which is to serve as a symbol for the totality of human experience must be complete. Although the tune is beyond us, it must not falsify, but play things as they are. The imagination heightens, orders, focuses, gives meaning —but does not lie or exclude inconvenient reality as myths, when worn out, too often have done. An anecdote from one of Stevens' letters to Henry Church indicates the nature of the leap of faith which the poet made in affirming the existence of a supreme fiction.

> One evening, a week or so ago, a student at Trinity College came to the office and walked home with me. We talked about this book [*Notes toward a Supreme Fiction*]. I said that I thought that we had reached a point at which we could no longer really believe in anything unless we recognized that it was a fiction. The student said that that was an impossibility, that there was no such thing as believing in something that one knew was not true. It is obvious, however, that we are doing that all the time. There are things with respect to which we willingly suspend disbelief; if there is instinctive in us a will to believe, or if there is a will to believe, whether or not it is in-

[4] Martz, "Wallace Stevens: The World as Meditation," p. 136.

stinctive, it seems to me that we can suspend disbelief with reference to a fiction as easily as we can suspend it with reference to anything else.[5]

As Stevens realized, any order or meaning which we find in the chaos of being must be imposed by the imagination, must, in short, be a fiction. And if we presume the existence of a world without the impressionistic distortions of the human senses, we must recognize that our presumption is still another fiction, for the first idea, too, is an imagined concept. To imagine reality without human imaginary tintings is just that—"to imagine." Thus, all perceptions of reality take the form of fictions, and, having accepted this, we know that we must nevertheless affirm, for the human condition is such that there is a passion for "yes" which underlies all our doubts. Stevens may recognize the "truth" of autumn, but in the face of that recognition he turns nonetheless to summer and its beauties, and believes in precisely that which he recognizes to be a fiction.

There are difficulties in exploring a poetry which relies so heavily upon explicit statement, for the poems themselves are so expository that ordinary explication is somewhat superfluous. One is left with the sometimes useful expedient of explaining one poem in terms of another, of glossing one image in the light of a similar image a few pages farther on. In this chapter I shall be more interested in attempting to show how the poems of *Transport to Summer* are parts which go "toward a supreme fiction" than in explication of individual poems.

Perhaps there is no clearer statement of Stevens' view of experience as process than that to be found in section VII of "Credences of Summer."

Three times the concentred self takes hold, three times
The thrice concentred self, having possessed

[5] Stevens, *Letters,* p. 430.

The object, grips it in savage scrutiny,
Once to make captive, once to subjugate
Or yield to subjugation, once to proclaim
The meaning of the capture, this hard prize,
Fully made, fully apparent, fully found.
(CP, p. 376)

The encounter of mind with world involves perception
(gripping and making captive), the struggle to make the
soil one's intelligence or in which the soil makes man *its*
intelligence (subjugating or yielding to subjugation), and
the ordering of and meditating upon the encounter which
gives it meaning and without which the "prize" of experience is not fully found. It is highly significant that "the
meaning of the capture" is "fully made." Any meaning
which we attribute to the interchange of mind and world is
a created meaning, a fiction "fully made" upon which everything depends. It is this third phase of experience, the
proclamation of the meaning of what has been captured by
the senses and subjugated by the reason, that produces the
supreme fiction. The original object "gripped in scrutiny" is
apotheosized by the imagination, and the result is the imagined land in which

Everything becomes morning, summer, the hero,
The enraptured woman, the sequestered night,
The man that suffered, lying there at ease
(CP, p. 378)

The "Pastoral Nun" realizes that "poetry" is the process by
which "a morning" becomes "the morning," and "a hero"
becomes "the hero." "Poetry and apotheosis are one," says
the nun, suggesting that poetry universalizes and tran-
scends "reality."

The idea of such poetic transformations is a matter,
Stevens believes, of "tight resemblances," in this poem resemblances between "something imagined and something
real." The poem "Thinking of a Relation between the Im-

ages of Metaphors" might have been written to illustrate the thesis that "poetry and apotheosis are one." The poem opens with a straight-forward statement about untransformed "reality." "The wood-doves are singing along the Perkiomen./ The bass lie deep, still afraid of the Indians" (CP, p. 356). The doves and the bass are multiple, particular, and literal. The river is highly particularized, given a proper name. The singing has been going on for some time, and the Indians who are "still" feared, perhaps the namers of the river, have almost certainly departed years ago.

> In the one ear of the fisherman, who is all
> One ear, the wood-doves are singing a single song. . . .
>
>   The fisherman is all
> One eye, in which the dove resembles the dove.
>   (CP, p. 356)

The fisherman, like the pastoral nun, is one gifted with the ability to see with the "inner" eye, hear with the "inner" ear. He perceives a resemblance between the imagined and the real, between the song of a single dove and the songs of many doves and between the vision of the divine or ideal dove and the sight of the particular dove.

The gifted fisherman is Stevens' own kind of Fisher King, the hero or the impossible-possible poet-philosopher who, having had time to think enough, grips the meaning of experience "fully made, fully apparent, fully found." The reader links Stevens' fisher by metaphorical resemblance to other fishers—Christ, the Apostolic fishers-of-men, Manu, the Buddha, Brons, and those noted American fishermen, Captain Ahab and his milder descendant, Ernest Hemingway's old man of *The Old Man and the Sea.*

As perceiver that the wood-doves' songs are as one song and that the bass resemble one another in that all look in one direction, the fisher sees that each dove, each bass, resembles the others; "There is one dove, one bass" (CP, p. 356). And Stevens, who is the director of the drama, sees that "there is one fisherman," although he may take many forms. Resemblance becomes the basis for a discovery of fundamental unity. The unification and intensification that result are both poetry and apotheosis. As Stevens puts it in "Three Academic Pieces," "the resemblance between things [is] one of the significant components of the structure of reality. It is significant because it creates [a relation among all things in nature]. It binds together" (NA, p. 72).

In "Thinking of a Relation between the Images of Metaphors," we find once again the idea of a "composition," a unity which the hero-poet might penetrate the chaos of "reality" to discover. To such a hero, "the dove/ Might spring to sight and yet remain a dove" (CP, p. 357). The dove as symbol of divinity and, more especially, the peace which passes understanding, is seen by the inner eye, and yet the particular earthly dove is not lost to sight. The object is not abandoned, but it is heightened, intensified. It is fully known and yet at the same time "fully made," for the mind of the fisherman apotheosizes the object it contemplates. Yet, the poem reminds us that the most brilliant creation of the mind depends upon the particular, for there it has its origin. As the title suggests, thinking of the relations between the images of metaphors is an act of creation which first unifies the particulars of the world and then transforms them into the heightened abstractions of poetry, into the supreme fiction.

The technique of *Transport to Summer* flows with apparent ease from fairly straightforward poetic statements of a thesis to more concrete illustrations of the thesis, as exemplified by "Thinking of a Relationship between the Images of Metaphors." By way of contrast, "Paisant Chronicle" is almost purely expository. Major man is not presented, but he is discussed in the abstract terms of the rational thought process.

> The major men—
> That is different. They are characters beyond

Reality, composed thereof. They are
The fictive men created out of men.
They are men but artificial men. . . .
(CP, p. 335)

Like "the dove" which resembles the dove of "reality," major man must be so rooted in actuality that he is "Nothing in which it is not possible/ To believe." The major men of fiction—Hamlet and Ahab and Don Quixote—are indeed composed of "reality," for the traits which they embody are shared to some extent by all men. However, in the degree to which our enduring fictional heroes possess the various traits which we attribute to them, they all are characters "beyond reality." Don Quixote, then, resembles many an idealist, but the idealist apotheosized is one of the major men, and can endure only as an artifice, one of the fictions which we accept as *true* in the full knowledge that it cannot be *real*.

But see him for yourself,
The fictive man. He may be seated in
A café. There may be a dish of country cheese
And a pineapple on the table. It must be so.
(CP, p. 335)

Only in the last stanza of "Paisant Chronicle" does Stevens place his major man in a concrete setting, and he does it by way of illustration. If he had set out to write a poem *of* major man rather than *about* major man, the setting would be quite ordinary. If the abstract figure is to be believed, he must be blooded; he must be found in familiar surroundings and move and speak in a world the mind can accept as possible. Ahab will forever be found on the blubber-smeared deck of a whaling ship and Don Quixote must forever ride across a landscape dotted with cheap inns and peopled with common humanity. Even major man must eat country cheese if he is to be believed in, and, according to Stevens, we can believe in nothing else.

One of Stevens' more fortuitous blendings of straightforward statement and concrete examples is the long meditative poem called "Description without Place." The poem begins with a statement—"It is possible that to seem—it is to be"—which, like the opening of a passage in good expository prose, establishes a thesis which Stevens is about to explore. The word *possible* is important to the tone and nature of the poem, for "Description without Place" is a meditation in which a mind pursues the course of a particular hypothesis through a series of tentative and qualified assertions. If we accept the proposition that seeming and being are one, then certain truths arise out of that acceptance.

In a sense, the entire poem is a dissertation on "seemings," a word which, for Stevens, denotes "the difference we make in what we see," the additions and subtractions that the imagination makes to and from "things as they are." Stevens says that there are two kinds of "seemings," actual seemings and potential seemings. Actual seemings are divided into "forward" and "backward" seemings, the former made up of "The way things look each day," and the latter "The greater seeming of the major mind" (CP, p. 340). Stevens uses, as he does so frequently, the sun to represent "things" in the physical universe. "The sun is an example. What it seems/ It is and in such seeming all things are" (CP, p. 339). The sun is a "savage seed," an "animal eye," "bull fire," Ulysses returning to Penelope, a "tuft of feathers," a "savage source," "Phoebus," the chariot of Phaeton, or a ball of flaming gases some 93,000,000 miles from the earth. Like the nature of everything else in the physical universe, the nature of the sun is determined by the human imagination's interaction with it. These are "forward seemings." "Backward seemings" are "greater" according to Stevens, and would seem closely related to the primordial archetypal images which Jung and others have postulated as being part of our racial consciousness. The major myths, the legends of the journey beneath the sea or of the search for the father or of miraculous transformation and rebirth or of god-men born to virgins, are fictive seemings which are the common property of all men. The "forward seemings," on the other hand, seem original and are created afresh continually.

What we call "cultural milieu" or what Whitehead terms "climate of opinion" is also a kind of "seeming."

> An age is a manner collected from a queen.
> An age is green or red. An age believes
>
> Or it denies. An age is solitude
> Or a barricade against the singular man
>
> By the incalculably plural.
>
> (CP, p. 340)

We do not, perhaps, realize the compression and power of Stevens' blank verse until we render the ideas it expresses into prose. Invariably the poetry has put the thought more effectively and more shortly. In the lines quoted above, the image of the queen represents an ordering principle, a central fiction around which the world falls into place. Such a queen once was Mary, virgin queen of Heaven, but, as Henry Adams for one knew, the virgin was no longer the central fiction for twentieth-century man. Later in "Description without Place" Stevens is to mention "Anne of England," a temporal queen whose world fell into place according to how it seemed to her, but by Stevens' time even temporal queens had lost most of their efficacy for creating an ordered world. Although Stevens does not wish to be taken too literally in his affirmation that a "queen" determines whether an age affirms or denies, it is interesting to consider the sort of queen who might represent our own age, surely an age which denies. She would seem to be the movie queen or beauty queen, those long-legged but curiously antiseptic creations which have come for us to be Venus and Diana, Isis and Mary.

Potential seemings are of four sorts: the seemings of the act of creation by a poet or other artist, the seemings of the familiar hero such as the soldier, the seemings which may (or may not) come into being in the future, and an immenser change which exists for Stevens only as a necessary postulate of the imagination. The poetry of the idea of these seemings is so difficult to divide from the idea that I shall quote Stevens at some length here.

> There are potential seemings, arrogant
> To be, as on the youngest poet's page,
>
> Or in the dark musician, listening
> To hear more brightly the contriving chords.
>
> There are potential seemings turbulent
> In the death of a soldier, like the utmost will,
>
> The more than human commonplace of blood,
> The breath that gushes upward and is gone,
>
> And another breath emerging out of death,
> That speaks for him such seemings as death gives.
>
> There might be, too, a change immenser than
> A poet's metaphors in which being would
>
> Come true, a point in the fire of music where
> Dazzle yields to a clarity and we observe,
>
> And observing is completing and we are content,
> In a world that shrinks to an immediate whole,
>
> That we do not need to understand, complete
> Without secret arrangements of it in the mind.
>
> (CP, pp. 340–41)

The first of these, the potential creations of the artist, would seem to need little explanation. The second, the potential seeming in the death of a soldier, is best explained by referring to other poems, for example, to "Gigantomachia" which insists that

> Each man himself became a giant,
> Tipped out with largeness, bearing the heavy

And the high, receiving out of others,
As from an inhuman elevation
And origin, an inhuman person,
A mask, a spirit, an accoutrement.
For soldiers, the new moon stretches twenty feet.

(CP, p. 289)

It is, of course, the breath of the poet which emerges from the death of the soldier and which speaks for the soldier as Homer, for example, speaks for Hector and as poets through the ages have spoken for the warrior and his larger than human sacrifice. The third kind of seeming is simply understood. There are, quite obviously, "seemings that are to be,/ Seemings that it is possible may be" (CP, p. 342). The change more immense than the poet's metaphors which Stevens postulates would be that change which would unite us with our world without need for so much as a tint of evading metaphor. We would perceive the world as an immediate whole, and would not be forced to impose an order upon chaotic reality; the "secret arrangements of [reality] in the mind" are fictions, seemings, which we choose, but the impossible-possible immense change would be a stasis, a contentment in a wholeness beyond our satisfactions with the unities we create. Stevens concludes section III of "Description without Place" with a catalog of historical figures who, by the strength of their minds, created seemings which became the seemings of an age.

Things are as they seemed to Calvin or to Anne
Of England, to Pablo Neruda in Ceylon,

To Nietzsche in Basel, to Lenin by a lake.
(CP, pp. 341–42)

Section IV then picks up the last two of these figures and examines them as examples of contrasting world views, as men to whom "things as they are" appeared to be very different. John Enck feels that Stevens disapproves of both Nietzsche and Lenin in their limited *Weltanschauung*.

The Russian and the German offer their distinctive aspects: Nietzsche in creating the *ubermensch* sought a single principle of the vertical; Lenin would have reduced all to identical flatness. . . . To avoid inflexibility one must practice at all times this multiple vision without an arid singularity of purpose, neither Nietzsche's nor Lenin's.[6]

I must disagree, for it seems to me that Nietzsche's imagination is the example Stevens uses to represent the fluid movement of the romantic mind, whereas Lenin's reason stands for the sterile fixing of life in a single abstract idea. Nietzsche masters motion, gilders the perpetual motion of the pool of the human mind, and in so doing serves as a figure to represent the romantic creative artist. Lenin, on the other hand, is the man of one idea, the "logical lunatic" of whom Stevens strongly disapproves. The one is the embodiment of the fluid, dynamic view of the world; the other embodies the fixed, mechanical view which rigidifies and thereby distorts nature.

Section V begins a series of equations in the form of definitions. "Seeming" is equal to "description without place." Section VI then goes a step further to indicate that "description is revelation."

> It is not
> The thing described, nor false facsimile.
>
> It is an artificial thing that exists,
> In its own seeming, plainly visible,
>
> Yet not too closely the double of our lives,
> Intenser than any actual life could be
>
> (CP, p. 344)

This poetry of abstract statement is illustrated in concrete form by another poem from *Transport to Summer*, "So-And-So Reclining on Her Couch." Stevens breaks the de-

---

[6] Enck, *Wallace Stevens*, p. 174.

scription of Mrs. Pappadopoulos into projections A, B, and C. Projection A is simply "This mechanism," the "thing described"; projection B is the "Idea" of the thing, the "false facsimile"; projection C is "the flux/ Between the thing as idea and/ The idea as thing. . . . [It is] half who made her" (CP, p. 295). The fictive creations are "intenser" than "actual life," and, being so, these reconciliations of mind and sun are highly significant.

> Thus the theory of description matters most.
> It is the theory of the word for those
>
> For whom the word is the making of the world, . . .
>
> It is a world of words to the end of it,
> In which nothing solid is its solid self.
>
> (CP, p. 345)

As Joseph Riddel has noted, section VII "circles back, as Stevens' meditations invariably do, to its beginning, and achieves an aesthetic whole. To seem is to be in the sense that poetry's seeming indeed *is* a reality in the mind of the beholder." [7]

All of this is saying exactly what Stevens has been saying no less directly in iambic pentameter. The major difference between the prosaic statements of critical paraphrase and Stevens' poetic statements is that Stevens does not attempt a rational, logical order, but rather follows the private associations and identifications of his mind. Riddel believes that "The esoteric and arbitrary byways into which his allusions take the reader are not altogether fortunate." [8] This might be true enough if the poet had intended "Description without Place" to stand alone, without reference to his body of work, and to be read without context. However, if the reader has steeped himself in the configurations of Stevens'

[7] Riddel, *Clairvoyant Eye*, p. 198.
[8] Ibid., p. 199.

poetic world, the allusions are neither so esoteric nor so arbitrary as Riddel suggests. The theory that underlies Stevens' poetic form is precisely that enunciated in "Description without Place." As one for whom the word is the making of the world, Stevens is describing and creating the world at the same time. Since creation is a process, and a highly personal process at that, the world he creates must take on the cast of his imagination, and the figures and symbols which appear in "Description without Place" are products of an evolution that begins with his earliest poems. The sun, the moon, Nietzsche, Lenin, motion, the dove, red, green—all are, by this time, familiar values in Stevens' work. These "symbols," if indeed they are symbols, have become as much a part of Stevens' processes of meditation as the iambic lines he uses with such freedom.

Perhaps the three most ambitious works in *Transport to Summer* are "Esthétique du Mal," "Notes toward a Supreme Fiction," and "Chocorua to Its Neighbor." Of the three, "Chocorua" is perhaps the most ambitious and at the same time the least successful poem. It is the most ambitious poem because, as John Enck notes, it is "As near a mystic vision as Stevens ventured," [9] and perhaps its lack of success is at least partly explained by Frank Kermode's complaint that "Chocorua . . . moves too slowly." [10] With all its faults, "Chocorua to Its Neighbor" is an important piece in Stevens' grand poem because it is the work in which the figure of major man has his longest speech (thirteen lines) and in which he is sketched most fully. As if Stevens does not trust himself to depict his own vision, he places the words of the poem in the "mouth" of what must be one of the most unusual dramatic personas in all literature— Mount Chocorua in New Hampshire. The mountain has seen a most unusual and most beautiful figure in the light

[9] Enck, *Wallace Stevens*, p. 170.
[10] Kermode, *Wallace Stevens*, p. 102.

of the morning star, and, awed by the apparition, it speaks to "its neighbor" to describe the "prodigious shadow" it has witnessed.

> He was a shell of dark blue glass, or ice,
> Or air collected in a deep essay,
> Or light embodied, or almost, a flash
> On more than muscular shoulders, arms and chest,
> Blue's last transparence as it turned to black. . . .
>
> (CP, p. 297)

Besides possessing immense size and great physical beauty, Stevens' hero is of the color signifying imagination and is the reconciler of the eternal opposites, fire and ice; the shell of blue ice contains a substance that is "like fire from an underworld/ Of less degree than flame and lesser shine" (CP, p. 297). In his ability to reconcile opposites, as in his mysterious origin and his beauty, Stevens' major man is reminiscent of Kubla Khan's stately pleasure dome, a well-known romantic symbol for the act of the imagination. Stevens' "total man" is perceived by Chocorua as "a flash" and his color is that precarious tint of blue that threatens to turn to black and thus disappear altogether into the night. "Poetry is a pheasant disappearing in the brush" (OP, p. 173), reads one of Stevens' *Adagia,* and that metaphor, like the metaphor of the figure described by Chocorua, emphasizes the evanescent nature of that momentary balance between external world and internal world, the balance which makes the poem. When the hero appears, beautiful and majestic, his lone action is that of seated meditation. He thinks aloud, and his thought is a process of self-definition.

> My solitaria
> Are the meditations of a central mind.
> I hear the motions of the spirit and the sound
> Of what is secret becomes, for me, a voice
> That is my own voice speaking in my ear.
>
> (CP, p. 298)

If "Chocorua" fails as poetry, and I think it does, perhaps it is because Stevens does not take his own advice about the presentation of the hero. The fictive man, as Stevens well knew, cannot be something in which it is impossible to believe. It is essential that the abstraction be blooded, that the hero appear in a believable, commonplace setting. The huge, shadowy figure which Chocorua describes does not grip the imagination because he is not composed of flesh and blood. Although the collective being knows that his likenesses, captains, cardinals, mothers and scholars, exist "under roof," neither he nor Stevens adequately expresses the truth that he is composed of such likenesses and has no existence without their existence. To encompass "mother" and "captain" in one figure, to present such a figure—even as a transparent shell of blue glass—is perhaps to try to "say more than human things with human voice," and, as Stevens himself says, "That cannot be" (CP, p. 300). The "mystic vision" cannot be directly presented; it must be translated into the images of day-to-day reality. Perhaps Stevens himself recognizes the failure of his presentation. Robert Pack suggests something of the crudeness of the hero in his evaluation of the concluding stanza of "Chocorua."

> The very last words of the poem are vague though suggestive. The word "rugged" suggests a crudeness, as if our conception of the hero was still undeveloped. The spirit of the last lines is one of beginning: it is dawn, in earliest winter. "Chocorua to Its Neighbor," terminating with three dots, does not really end, but anticipates the next poem, the newest imagining of the hero.[11]

Thus, in the ending of "Chocorua" is its beginning; the voice of the mountain is discarded, and Stevens begins again the search for the proper symbolic representation of the infinite possibility of man and his imagination. The

[11] Pack, *Wallace Stevens*, p. 164.

other two long poems of *Transport to Summer*, "Esthétique du Mal" and "Notes toward a Supreme Fiction" may be seen as new attempts to compose human experience in a suitable symbolic form.

In a letter to John Crowe Ransom, Stevens indicated that a letter quoted by Ransom in an article called "Artists, Soldiers, Positivists" in *Kenyon Review* had aroused the poet's interest in "the relation between poetry and what [the letter writer] called pain." [12] The quoted letter, apparently written by an American soldier sometime in 1944, had criticized the poetry of *Kenyon Review* as being "cut off from pain."

> It is intellectual and it is fine, but it never reveals muscle and nerve. It does not really matter whether poetry of men in war, or suffering the impact of communiqués, has a large or small "frame of reference." It must, I feel, promise survival for all who are worth saving—it must communicate a lot of existence; an overwhelming desire to go on. . . . I'm waiting for an American poem of the forties called "The Quip at the Heart of the Debacle." . . . The conditions for approach to the poem will be baptism by fire. [13]

Stevens commented, "Whatever he may mean, it might be interesting to do an esthétique du mal. It is the kind of idea that it is difficult to shake off." [14] In many ways, the problem of the relation between poetry and pain was an idea which Stevens had not "shaken off" since he began publishing poetry, for "Esthétique du Mal" is very like "Sunday Morning," the great poem of *Harmonium*, in both tone and subject matter. I feel certain that the letter in *Kenyon Review* had little to do with the form that Stevens' poem

[12] Stevens, *Letters*, p. 468.
[13] Ransom, "Artists, Soldiers, Postivists," 276–77.
[14] Stevens, *Letters*, p. 468.

took; all that remains of the soldier's plea for "The Quip at the Heart of the Debacle" is Stevens' commitment to the acceptance of the totality of existence, an acceptance which forever precludes the possibility of being "cut off from pain." To look long and steadily at the central *mal* of the human condition does constitute a kind of "baptism by fire," and Stevens had been preparing for his "Esthétique" for almost a quarter of a century. It is necessary that the "Esthétique du Mal" precede "Notes toward a Supreme Fiction" because the supreme fiction must embrace the central evil if it is to reach the central good; because if Satan is dead, we must find a new myth to enable us to endure the pain of our condition; because it is in the human condition that the need for the supreme fiction arises. Our universal *mal* creates the conditions from which the poem springs.

It is interesting to note both the similarities and the differences between "Sunday Morning," the *Harmonium* poem of the acceptance of the physical universe, and "Esthétique du Mal," the counterpart poem of *Transport to Summer*. Each begins with a dramatic persona, a figure who sits in the midst of comfortable surroundings and contemplates an "old catastrophe." However, the woman of the *Harmonium* poem is involved in a kind of constant dialog of self and soul, a dialog in which questions and their answers make up the poem, while the masculine voice of "Esthétique du Mal" is heard and then is not heard from section to section of the poem. Stevens has taken his own advice from the earlier poem, "Of Modern Poetry," in which he asserts that the modern poem has

> To construct a new stage. It has to be on that stage
> And, like an insatiable actor, slowly and
> With meditation, speak words that in the ear,
> In the delicatest ear of the mind, repeat,
> Exactly, that which it wants to hear, at the sound
> Of which, an invisible audience listens,

> Not to the play, but to itself, expressed
> In an emotion as of two people, as of two
> Emotions becoming one. . . .
>   (CP, p. 240)

The stage setting for "Esthétique du Mal" is Naples, and the actor is writing letters home and reading paragraphs on the sublime; his emotions are evoked by his setting, and his meditations in turn evoke the same emotion in his "invisible audience." Unlike "Sunday Morning," in which the action moves from the protagonist's misgivings about the impermanence of the physical beauty of the earth, her desire for "imperishable beauty," to an acceptance of the universe as it is, an acceptance which includes the idea that "Death is the mother of beauty," "Esthétique du Mal" is a series of meditative assertions, each of which is pursued and examined with a minimum of dependence upon the other segments of the poem. While earlier poems, such as "Sunday Morning," present a dramatic and fairly steady movement toward a resolution, "Esthétique du Mal" pursues a much more varied course, for its movement is patterned after the shifting rhythms and moods of meditation. The poems in the series are joined only by a common concern with the need to accept the *mal* of our existence as part of the sublime.

The freedom of the internal monologue which is the form of "Esthétique du Mal" is reflected in the irregularity of the stanza length in the poem. "Sunday Morning" is composed of eight numbered stanzas of fifteen lines each. "Esthétique du Mal" is divided into irregular "sections" consisting of anywhere from one stanza to seven stanzas. The stanzas themselves vary in length from the familiar tercets which Stevens employs in "Notes toward a Supreme Fiction" to an unbroken stanza of twenty-five lines. Moreover, the sections may be as long as twenty-six lines or as short as twenty-one.

The sections also vary in rhyming technique, for while

most employ no rhyme at all, section III uses exact rhyme and near rhyme effectively.

> His firm stanzas hang like hives in hell
> Or what hell was, since now both heaven and hell
> Are one, and here, O terra infidel.
>
> (CP, p. 315)

These exact, repetitive, and almost jingling rhymes are nicely balanced by the subtle repetitions of accented vowel and consonant sounds in the closing tercet.

> As if hell, so modified, had disappeared,
> As if pain, no longer satanic mimicry,
> Could be borne, as if we were sure to find our way.
>
> (CP, p. 316)

These rhymes are almost beyond auditory range, but there is an echo of "mimicry" in "our way," and there is an internal alliteration in the "s" sounds of "so modified," "satanic," and "sure to find." Stevens' use of rhyme and off rhyme, near rhyme and no rhyme at all, in the same poem indicates the freedom he has attained in the use of his medium.

Marked changes in tone, reinforced by variations in rhyme and in meter, seem most deliberate on Stevens' part, and perhaps suggest the ever-shifting movement of the mind in its meditations. Our plight is seen as now comic, now tragic, first pleasant, then bitter; the patient syllables must reflect the kaleidoscopic nuances of meditation, for meditation, like life, is motion.

The poems within "Esthétique du Mal" are occasionally dramatic, but for the most part they begin with a thesis—a poetic thesis, one that is presented in concrete images rather than in abstract terms—and then pursue the implications of that thesis by expanding the images and commenting upon them. For example, section VI begins with the image of "The sun in clownish yellow, but not a clown"; section VII begins with the famous "How red the rose that is the soldier's wound"; and section XI begins with the even more famous "Life is a bitter aspic. We are not/ At the centre of a diamond" (CP, p. 322). Each of these images enlarges to become a dissertation on the evil of our condition. "A big bird," probably the bird of time, pecks with insatiable appetite at the sun of "clownish yellow" to represent the failing of the perfection of each day, the *mal* of mutability. "The red rose" of the soldier's wound comes to be the beautiful emblem of "all/ The soldiers that are falling," and hence, emblem of all suffering and pain. The soldier becomes all men, for war is undoubtedly the supreme symbol of death and evil for twentieth-century man. "At dawn,/ The paratroopers fall and as they fall/ They mow the lawn." We live, Stevens was to say in "Notes toward a Supreme Fiction," in a place that is not our own; we are not at the center of the diamond, and the falling paratroopers, the sinking ship, and the graves of the departed and unsentimentalized "dishonest" poor represent the incomprehensible violence and essential bitterness of human life. Yet, bird and rose and bitter aspic are all raw material from which Stevens can fashion "So many selves, so many sensuous worlds," for it is precisely from mutability and human pain and the bitterness of our alienation in the only land we possess that the poem arises. "Natives of poverty, children of malheur,/ The gaiety of language is our seigneur" (CP, p. 322). In each of these sections, there is a reconciliation, a revolving of the bird toward immense perfections, the stroking of the head of the soldier of time who finds his wound good because life is good, the caressing tongue of the man of bitter appetite on the "exacerbations" of life's bitter aspic. Generally speaking, each section of "Esthétique" begins with the evil of our condition and ends with a reconciliation to and acceptance of that evil. "The death of Satan" may be a tragedy, but the section (VIII) which opens with his destruction concludes with an affirmation of man's "passion for yes." "It may be that one life is a punishment/ For another" (XIII), but there is still the possibility that a man may "establish the visible" and call "a zone of blue and orange/ Versicolorings" "The ultimate good." We begin each section of the poem in purgatorial fire, but usually end with flowers. If the flowers happen to be roses with pain-filled thorns or violets growing on graves, they are beautiful and compensatory nonetheless. The fires of Vesuvius and the roses in the café are—as Eliot, for one, would have known—one, for suffering and beauty, mal and esthétique, are inseparable.

The final stanza of the "Esthétique," like that of "Sunday Morning," is a celebration of the beauties of the physical universe. However, while "Sunday Morning" begins section VIII with a continuation of the dramatic movement of the poem, the concluding section of "Esthétique du Mal" begins with an abstract statement, a kind of thesis. There is no return to the nameless "he" who writes letters in the opening of the poem. Both poems conclude with lovely images of the affluence of our planet, but "Sunday Morning" presents the earth in straightforward fashion, while "Esthétique" presents a vision of the earth as it "might" be seen by "non-physical" people after death. The gleaming corn is seen as through the refracting lens of imagined possibility, a lens which intensifies and beautifies because the non-physical people are forever separated from the beauty which they see too late.

> Perhaps,
> After death, the non-physical people, in paradise,
> Itself non-physical, may, by chance, observe
> The green corn gleaming and experience
> The minor of what we feel. The adventurer
> In humanity has not conceived of a race
> Completely physical in a physical world.
> (CP, p. 325)

The completely physical exists only as a necessary postulate of the mind, a possibility which represents an extreme pole in the range of the flowing interchange of the world and the imagination. As Stevens puts it,

> out of what one sees and hears and out
> Of what one feels, who could have thought to make
> So many selves, so many sensuous worlds,
> As if the air, the mid-day air, was swarming
> With the metaphysical changes that occur,
> Merely in living as and where we live.
>
> (CP, p. 326)

This delight in the changing world is our compensation for "living as and where we live," for the *mal* at the heart of our condition. We are condemned to be alienated from our physical environment and to be imprisoned in the cycle of change and decay, but in this thesis we find "delight," for the constant flow of things of the earth and of our feelings interact to produce the "reverberating psalm, the right chorale" (CP, p. 326).

The *Letters of Wallace Stevens,* a collection which might be subtitled "or why new critics grow old," is the safest starting point for a discussion of "Notes toward a Supreme Fiction." Stevens was particularly willing to explicate his own lines, and his letters to Hi Simons and Henry Church about "Notes" constitute a lengthy exercise in critical analysis. "I am always taken by surprise by the particular things that people find obscure," he wrote Henry Church, "But, after all, one's own symbols may not be everyone's." [15]

Of greater significance, surely, than his glossing of individual figures and lines ("the Canon Asprin is simply a figure, not a symbol. This name is supposed to suggest the kind of person he is.") [16] are Stevens' statements of his over-all intention in creating "Notes toward a Supreme Fiction." On January 12, 1943, he wrote to Hi Simons,

[15] Ibid., p. 427.
[16] Ibid.

I ought to say that I have not defined a supreme fiction A man as familiar with my things as you are will be justified in thinking that I mean poetry. I don't want to say I don't mean poetry; I don't know what I mean. The next thing for me to do will be to try to be a little more precise about this enigma. I hold off from even attempting that because, as soon as I start to rationalize, I lose the poetry of the idea. In principle, there appear to be certain characteristics of a supreme fiction *and the NOTES is confined to a statement of a few of those characteristics.* . . . In trying to create something as valid as the idea of God has been, and for that matter remains, the first necessity seems to be breadth. It is true that the thing would never amount to much until there is no breadth, or rather, until it has all come to a point.[17]

A little more than two weeks later, he added, "I think I said in my last letter to you that the Supreme Fiction is not poetry, but I also said that I don't know what it is going to be. Let us think about it and not say that our abstraction is this, that or the other." [18]

However, another letter, this one to Henry Church, seems to me most revealing concerning the relationship between supreme fiction and poetry.

I have no idea of the form that a supreme fiction would take. The NOTES start out with the idea that it would not take any form: that it would be abstract. Of course, in the long run, poetry would be the supreme fiction; *the essence of poetry is change and the essence of change is that it gives pleasure* [italics mine].[19]

The last sentence strikes me as one of the most significant prose statements Stevens ever made about the nature of poetry. The essence of poetry is change because poetry is

[17] Ibid., p. 435.
[18] Ibid., p. 438.
[19] Ibid., p. 430.

the abstract (in Stevens' sense of "universalized") figure for life, and life is change. Poetry, like dance, is a series of movements, of ever-shifting accents and rhythms flowing naturally out of rhythms and into still newer rhythms. It is a process which includes the flux of resemblances, the locus of metamorphosized points of resemblance which can be derived from so common an object as a glass of water. Poetry is the creation of images and symbols which never stay fixed in value, but which continually take on new and different significances as their contexts shift from poem to poem. And, as Stevens surely realized by 1943, to write poetry over a lifetime or a part of a lifetime is to keep a record of change, a record of dominant themes becoming recessive and of themes which emerge, evolve, and disappear or survive. The essence of Stevens' poetry is, indeed, change. And, just as change is what delights us on the earth, so, too, as Stevens says, it is the changing nature of poetry which delights us in it.

I shall not attempt to explicate "Notes toward a Supreme Fiction" in any ordered fashion.[20] Rather, my concern is with the place of that poem in the total scheme of Stevens' work. Although the poem had been written before most of the works which comprise *Transport to Summer*, Stevens insists that "Notes" be the final poem of the volume. Obviously it was intended, for the moment, to be a kind of summing up, a number of short poems which discussed and at the same time embodied the necessary qualities of a fiction which might be "as valid as the idea of God." "Notes toward a Supreme Fiction" is not, as Stevens' comments and the title itself make clear, meant to *be* the supreme fiction; however, neither the tone of the poem nor the author's remarks concerning the poem indicate that he viewed

[20] In addition to Stevens' own comments on "Notes," I recommend the studies of Nassar, pp. 179–217; Riddel, pp. 167–85 of *Clairvoyant Eye;* Enck, pp. 161–69; Doggett, pp. 98–115 of *Poetry of Thought;* and especially Harold Bloom's excellent article, " 'Notes toward a Supreme Fiction': A Commentary," pp. 76–95.

it as mere "preparation," as a kind of outline for a major poem which he intended to write in the future. It would seem that "Notes toward a Supreme Fiction" uses the preposition *toward* in the same way that one uses it when he speaks of "parts toward a whole." These short poems, because they contain the qualities necessary to produce a supreme fiction, are worthy to be considered fragments of such a fiction.

Perhaps we can believe Stevens when he says that he does not know what he means by a supreme fiction, but surely the world of his *Collected Poems* came to be for him his "imagined land," his "planet on the table," and just as surely he became more conscious of this fact in the poetry which follows *Transport to Summer*. "In the long run," indeed, poetry, *his* poetry, fulfills his requirements for a supreme fiction. It is his own world, different from the physical, yet dependent upon it and evolving from it; it is universalized, concerned with the idea of man and the idea of the vital abstraction; it changes constantly, as we have seen, from the sensory world of *Harmonium* to the musing meditations of the later work; and, above all, it brings pleasure, not only to the reader but to the creator, for, as Stevens himself puts it,

> We enjoy the ithy oonts and long-haired
> Plomets, as the Herr Gott
> Enjoys his comets.
> (CP, p. 349)

"On the mid-day of the year," at mid-summer, the marriage of the great captain and the maiden Bawda can take place, and then only in the Carolinas, Stevens' meeting place of north and south. In the marriages of "Notes," Stevens produces a momentary stasis, an acceptance of summer in its savagest diamonds before turning, as he must, to "True autumn" standing in the doorway. The final poem of *Transport to Summer* is the unfolding of the "azure-doubled crimsons" of that season. "Each false thing ends," Stevens had said;

> The bouquet of summer
> Turns blue and on its empty table
> It is stale and the water is discolored.
> (CP, p. 280)

One looks, and the bouquet is gone, but the air is aswarm with the auroras of autumn.

The Auroras of Autumn

With the falling leaves and darkening colors of *Auroras of Autumn*, Wallace Stevens' poetry reaches the end of the inward journey which began fourteen years before with the publication of *Ideas of Order*. In each volume, *Auroras* and *Ideas of Order*, Stevens uses the image of the snake sloughing its skin and that of the abandoned cabin on the beach. The first is, of course, a traditional symbol of change and rebirth, and the second suggests a mental dwelling place, an idea in which one has lived for a time but which has now been left behind. It would appear that, just as in 1936 Stevens may have realized that the hedonist's progress was the way only to dusty death, so, in 1950, having asked what man can ultimately know, he had discovered that the answer seemed to be that man can know only the shapes formed in his own mind. "Notes toward a Supreme Fiction" has struck a momentary balance, a marriage of imagination and phenomenal world, but such a balance occurs as it occurs, and with midsummer past the scale tips and the world of objects becomes a little hard to see as Stevens descends deeper and deeper into the world of the mind.

In *Auroras of Autumn*, the last independently published volume before the collection which suggested a final reckoning, Stevens has come, according to Leslie Fiedler, to write "poetry about poetry about poetry." One might put the same thought in another, less pejorative, way by saying that in his final volumes Stevens is writing about the processes by which man comes to know, or, more properly, about the nature of our experience in our world. That this is also poetry about poetry about poetry is true enough; as always for Stevens, the theory of poetry is the theory of life. The heart of that theory is still the relationship between mind and soil, but by this time Stevens is interested in the relationship itself, not with the mind or with the soil in and of themselves. If "being," our experience, is not something occurring in the mind, where does it occur? In what sense is there such a thing as "being," and, equally important, in what way can the artist present such an elusive concept?

To find the answer, Stevens examines the mind's own processes, and the result is a poetry which is increasingly symbolic, personal, associative, and meditative—and, correspondingly, less dramatic and external. Soil and intelligence are still present forces in this verse, but they no longer have significant existence anywhere but in Stevens' meditations. These vital poles in Stevens' work give way to mere symbols of themselves, counters which move easily and rapidly—much more easily and rapidly than it was possible to manipulate the Carolinas and Crispin's mind. By this time, colors, physical phenomena such as sun and moon, and personas such as queens and soldiers are so rigidified as symbols that they almost lose their values as parts of the phenomenal world. Indeed, Stevens seems scarcely to concern himself with his counters except as counters—pawns in an intellectual game with an understanding of the nature of being as the stake.

As Stevens' poetry becomes more and more meditative, internalized verse, the poems take on a new kind of dynamism. This poetry does not have the lusty quality of *Harmonium*, but, as the subject matter becomes more abstract, and as the opposing forces involved become more and more symbolic, the sense of movement between those opposites becomes increasingly acute. Perhaps because the action is totally contained in the mind, and the thoughts move more swiftly than Crispin ever could, the flickerings between mind and objective world become more rapid than ever before. Stevens seems finally to conclude that being or life is captured only when the oscillation between mind and world is so rapid that the two blur for an instant into a seemingly solid image. The "solid" is a fiction because the movement can take place only in the mind of the man in meditation, a poetic action in Stevens' terms. The poet, thinking about what experience is, finds that the poem is a flickering thing existing in the motion between the external world and the mind.

The auroras are, therefore, perfect figures for poetry as Stevens conceived it—bright flickerings in the darkness, constantly changing with each appearance, most rare and most beautiful. They surpass similar images which Stevens tries elsewhere, yet all are images of quick bright things which disappear almost before a man can see and cry "Behold." "A poem is a meteor," writes Stevens in one of the *Adagia* (OP, p. 158), and the metaphor, like that of the disappearing pheasant, is designed to accentuate the evanescence of poetry.

The problem of defining the poem, then, is once again the problem of defining life for the romantic artist. Such a man, trying to create a symbol of the truth about human life, knows from the outset that if the truth is dynamic and organic it will not hold still in the material with which he must work, for clay, words, and paint must all take fixed patterns. And such patterns, he knows only too well, are false to the essential, dynamic nature of existence.

Thus Stevens finds himself in the position of trying to find an image to suggest the flickering impermanence of the present moment as it disappears, meteor-like, into the past. "And yet what good were yesterday's devotions?" Stevens asks with a sigh. "I affirm and then at midnight the great cat/ Leaps quickly from the fireside and is gone" (CP, p. 264). For Stevens, the intersection of past and future is catlike—swift, silent, and forever untamable.

The Auroras of Autumn employs a very large number of varied images designed to suggest the flowing impermanence of experience. In addition to the serpent of the title poem "flashing without form," there is the "angel of reality,/ Seen for a moment standing in the door." The angel is the "necessary angel" because only he can clear the sight of its "stiff and stubborn, man-locked set." Here, too, the idea of the earth cannot be "stiff" or "fixed" if reality is to be apprehended. The angel, like the great cat, "lasts only for the blink of an eye":

> Am I not,
> Myself, only half of a figure of a sort,
>
> A figure half seen, or seen for a moment, a man
> Of the mind, an apparition apparelled in
>
> Apparels of such lightest look that a turn
> Of my shoulder and quickly, too quickly, I am gone?
> (CP, p. 497)

That the "angel of reality" should be "a man/ Of the mind" suggests that "reality" may be only a necessary postulate of the imagination, that even the idea of things untainted by metaphor is a consequence of the way we feel, not of the things themselves.

The conclusion of that dissertation on the nature of the real, "An Ordinary Evening in New Haven," is that

> It is not in the premise that reality
> Is a solid. It may be a shade that traverses
> A dust, a force that traverses a shade.
> (CP, p. 489)

In this case, reality is suggested to be comprised of a movement or energy without form, a movement too rapid to be seen as a solid. The examples could be multiplied:

The bouquet stands in a jar, as metaphor,
As lightning itself is, likewise, metaphor
Crowded with apparitions suddenly gone

And no less suddenly here again, a growth
Of the reality of the eye, an artifice,
Nothing much, a flitter that reflects itself.

(CP, p. 448)

Or, one might examine "The Woman in Sunshine," a form-less, imageless person who is

More definite for what she is—

Because she is disembodied,
Bearing the odors of the summer fields,

Confessing the taciturn and yet indifferent,
Invisibly clear, the only love.

(CP, p. 445)

There is also the Platonic, impossible poem "at the centre of things" (which might be Stevens' way of tracing the ideal symbol for being) which is described in this way:

It is and it
Is not and, therefore, is. In the instant of speech,
The breadth of an accelerando moves,
Captives the being, widens—and was there.

(CP, p. 440)

Or again, one might examine the symbol which Stevens chooses for being in his "Metaphor as Degeneration."

It is being.
That is the flock-flecked river, the water,
The blown sheen—or is it air?

How, then, is metaphor degeneration,
When Swatara becomes this undulant river
And the river becomes the landless, waterless ocean?

(CP, p. 444)

Being is a flowing, neither water nor air nor fire nor earth, a half-seen form snatched from the blurred passage of pres-

The Auroras of Autumn   123

And its tawny caricature and tawny life,
Another thought, the paramount ado . . .
Since what we think is never what we see.

(CP, pp. 459–60)

The violet tintings of the imagination, successfully resisted by the bright light of morning, deepen as the afternoon wears on. The pattern of changing images suggests the progression of any experience as it moves from sensation to thought, memory, and meditation. Finally, the moment of sensory experience, the vivid green of the morning trees, degenerates into one of the forms in which we fix and falsify our being—"the pedestal," "the ambitious page," the "scrawl," and "the pyramid." All of these forms are flawed in some way, are either dog-eared or tawny, are merely caricatures of experience, the result of a process of re-creation.

It should be noted that Stevens here has presented in a dynamic, organic form the equivalent of dynamic, organic experience. The poem changes, as does experience, and changes from concrete images taken from nature and drawn in vivid blues and greens to the gray violet shadows of images drawn from artifacts. Only by presenting the poem as mental drama, as a struggle between opposites in which one opposite evolves out of the other and is dependent upon it, can Stevens capture in poetry the dramatic, moving nature of experience. By the time we formalize the event, put it on the pedestal or the ambitious page, indeed "what we think" is far removed from the things we saw "before noon." But by presenting the event as *process*, Stevens comes closer to capturing the flavor of experience than does the artist who attempts to reproduce life in a static form.

Another poem which illustrates, though less dynamically, the nature of "things as they are" is the pleasant "Questions Are Remarks." As in "What We See Is What We Think," the poem juxtaposes the immediate sensory view of experience with the caricatures presented by the mind in its meditations. The difference is that in "Questions" the two views are presented in dramatic conflict rather than as poles in a process. Peter, aged two, represents the pure sensory experiencer. The "drowsy, infant, old men," and Peter's mother represent those who have lost that untainted vision and replaced it with the "forms" which are traditional ways of viewing reality. Since Peter is a grandson, aged two, the implication that the grandfather has been Peter and that Peter will one day be a drowsy, sleepy old man is inescapable. The process of experience is implicit in the poem, although the poem does not reproduce that process as does "What We See Is What We Think." Peter's question-remark, Stevens tells us, is

> complete because it contains
> His utmost statement. It is his own array,
> His own pageant and procession and display,

> As far as nothingness permits . . .
>   (CP, pp. 462–63)

In short, Peter's question is more a statement of wonder than an attempt to gain information. The mother's answer, on the other hand, makes use of outworn forms, the mythology of the "red horse," a vision which has no vitality and no relation to the question Peter has asked. The object in question, the sun, arises "with so much rhetoric," an example of the "dog-eared," or "tawny," view of experience. Neither question nor answer reaches that delicate balance-point at which the truth might be realized. Peter's perception must mingle with the blue of the imagination to produce for a moment the poetic vision which reveals "the way of things." However, as Miller has said, in the rapid movement between opposites the poet touches something close to things as they are. Peter sees the sun almost "as it is" but cannot speak the word; he is seer and potential poet, but can produce an "utmost statement" only as far "as nothing-ness permits." The old men are prisoners of "the antique acceptances," hopelessly removed from their mother-earth, completely outside of the realm of perception and given over to meditation in its place. Peter has the perceptions, but not the means to articulate them as a stay against disintegrations; the old men have the forms with which to articulate their condition and the way of experience, but they are those for whom "what is seen is never what is thought," and their question, unlike Peter's, reflects uncer-tainty and a sense of loss. The sun does not pierce their vision, and the disintegrations of late afternoon show them to be as infantile as Peter. The human condition is such that man finds himself between the horns of a metaphysical dilemma. On the one hand, sensory experience is meaning-less, incomplete, totally incomprehensible, until it is given a form and an order by the mind; on the other, once experi-ence is given a form and order, that form and order are *not* the experience—indeed, they transform the experience into a fiction. However, in articulating the nature of the di-lemma itself, in "thinking about what it is to think," the artist also makes a statement about the quality and texture of "being" as we experience it.

In *The Auroras of Autumn* Stevens makes use of two very dissimilar figures in his attempt to present the nature of being. The figures are those of an ever-flowing river and, strangely enough, a bouquet of flowers—a still life. The use of the river for such a purpose is a traditional enough one. We speak of "the flowing of time" almost as casually as we refer to a "field of study," quite unaware in most cases of the metaphorical nature of the phrase. In *Auroras,* the most obvious uses of the river as symbol are found in "The Solitude of Cataracts" and in "Metaphor as Degeneration." In the former, the Heraclitean paradox about man's inabil-ity to step twice into the same river is given a subjective twist by Stevens.

He never felt twice the same about the flecked river,
Which kept flowing and never the same way twice, flowing

Through many places, as if it stood still in one, . . .
(CP, p. 424)

The changing nature of the river is implicit in Stevens, as it
was in Heraclitus, but of greater significance is the power
of the imagination which flows as rapidly as the river and
which keeps the "He" of the poem (and, by extension, any
man) from any certainty or fixed emotional state. The
conflict of "Solitude of Cataracts" is that between the
changing nature of "things as they are" and man's desire for
permanence.

He wanted to feel the same way over and over.

He wanted the river to go on flowing the same way,
To keep on flowing. He wanted to walk beside it,

Under the buttonwoods, beneath a moon nailed fast.
He wanted his heart to stop beating and his mind to rest

In a permanent realization, without any wild ducks
Or mountains that were not mountains, just to know how
it would be,

Just to know how it would feel, released from destruction, . . .
(CP, p. 425)

The changing nature of the world is implicit in the moon,
the "fluttering" ducks, the mountains which the imagination changes into other things, the flowing river. The dramatic persona of the poem has a very human, very natural
desire to come to certainty and order, a desire born of
awareness that the flow of the river and the flow of the
circulatory system belong to the process of destruction; life
may be motion, but one may be excused a moment of
motion sickness now and then.

"Metaphor as Degeneration" explicitly identifies the flowing river with the concept of being. Here the action is the imagination's apotheosis of the Swatara river in Connecticut to the embodiment of the age-old concept of the river of time. Doggett has pointed to Stevens' association of the Swatara with the river Styx, not only in this poem, but in others as well, and the comparison is apt.[4] As in "Solitude of Cataracts," the flowing river calls up unmistakable reminders of mortality.

> Here the black violets grow down to its banks
> And the memorial mosses hang their green
> Upon it, as it flows ahead.
> (CP, p. 445)

The end of the flow of being is, for the individual, nonbeing, as Stevens well knew. Nonetheless, if being includes death, it also includes the imagination. In this poem Stevens sets the one off against the other as if they are opposing forces, the black and the white of the flow of things.

> If there is a man white as marble
> Sits in a wood, in the greenest part,
> Brooding sounds of the images of death,
>
> So there is a man in black space
> Sits in nothing that we know,
> Brooding sounds of river noises;
>
> And these images, these reverberations,
> And others, make certain how being
> Includes death and the imagination.
> (CP, p. 444)

The river that flows through matter and produces physical change flows also through the mind and produces the creative activity of the imagination. If the one flow is destructive, a "degeneration," in the metamorphoses that it produces, the other, the flow of the imagination, is such that its metamorphoses are apotheosizing rather than degenerative.

[4] Doggett, *Stevens' Poetry of Thought*, p. 69.

The man "white as marble" who sits in greenest reality musing on the nature of change sees it as the agent of physical degeneration. The man "in black space" who— poet-fashion—broods on "sounds of river noises" sees the changing nature of the imagination (the will to change) as the force which elevates the commonplace by investing it with abstract and symbolic significance.

It is certain that the river

Is not Swatara. . . . It is being. . . .

How, then, is metaphor degeneration,
When Swatara becomes this undulant river
And the river becomes the landless, waterless ocean?
(CP, p. 444)

Change, then, has two forms—the destructive flow of being over physical matter which brings decay, and the creative flow of being through the mind which elevates, delights, and gives meaning and value to human experience.

To emphasize the constantly changing resemblances which the mind half-creates and half-perceives, Stevens uses the inert figure of the bouquet of flowers. Since the bouquet is a still life and apparently not involved in physical flux, the changes which the poet makes in it, the changes of his "sense of things," must be entirely within his mind. In "Bouquet of Roses in Sunlight," Stevens begins by insisting that the bouquet is "too actual" to be changed by metaphor.

Say that it is a crude effect, black reds,
Pink yellows, orange whites, too much as they are
To be anything else in the sunlight of the room,

Too much as they are to be changed by metaphor,
Too actual, things that in being real
Make any imaginings of them lesser things.
(CP, p. 430)

As noted earlier, Stevens had come to realize that even the failure of metaphor before the strength of reality is a part of our sense of things; the absence of imagination has, itself, to be imagined.

> And yet this effect is a consequence of the way
> We feel and, therefore, is not real, except
> In our sense of it, our sense of the fertilest red . . .
> (CP, p. 430)

Our sense of things, the way we feel, is a flowing and that flowing produces changes in our experience of being which are beyond the changes wrought by either metaphor or altered slantings of the sun's light.

To tell more than the truth about the bouquet, to be the rhetorician, is to make the flowers lesser things. (One thinks of Robert Frost's line from "Mowing": "Anything more than the truth would have seemed too weak . . ."). But the changes in our sense of them are like changes in meaning, changes that take place beyond the level of a rhetoric, indeed that defy verbalization. They are like, Stevens says, "a flow of meanings with no speech" (CP, p. 431). Even the crude effect of untransformed reality is part of a flowing, not an absolute, but part of a process which, like the river, is moving in all places at once, even though it may seem to stand still in whatever place is scrutinized by a given beholder at a given moment.

"The Bouquet," another and longer treatment of the paradox of the flowing still life, begins with a passage celebrating the flickering nature of reality. A bouquet is an artifice, an arrangement, and as artifice it is not itself in "flux" but is "Suspended in temporary jauntiness" (CP, p. 448). Works of art, things "of medium nature," are thought by "meta-men" to be things "transfixed, transpierced," and the meta-men's conception of these things is ultimately false in Stevens' scheme of values. In the world of meta-men,[5] life is

[5] Eugene Nassar thinks them "rationalists." See his *Wallace Stevens,* p. 98.

perceived with remarkable fixity. "A pack of cards is falling toward the floor./ The sun is secretly shining on the wall" (CP, p. 450).

The transfixed cards, arrested in mid-air, are "queered" by the "lavishings" of the "will to see" of the meta-men. Just so, the flowers in the jar are turned "para-things" and are made "farced, finikin" by the "angular" world view of the cold meta-men.

> They are not splashings in a penumbra. They stand.
> They are. The bouquet is a part of the dithering:
> Cloud's gold, of a whole appearance that stands and is.
>
> (CP, p. 452)

The brief concluding section presents a striking change in tone and technique. Suddenly Stevens employs the dramatic mode, and the meditative tone disappears.

> A car drives up. A soldier, an officer,
> Steps out. He rings and knocks. The door is not locked.
> He enters the room and calls. No one is there.
> He bumps the table. The bouquet falls on its side.
> He walks through the house, looks round him and then
>   leaves.
> The bouquet has slopped over the edge and lies on the floor.
>
> (CP, pp. 452–53)

The short, choppy sentences, the repetitions of subject and active verb, suggest rapid movement and life as a process of events leading one into the other. The fact that the protagonist is a soldier is, perhaps, significant, for Eugene Nassar has suggested that in Stevens' mythology the soldier is the figure who "fights his continual 'war' against emptiness and chaos or against false abstraction and outworn fictions." [6] In this poem, the soldier is a part of the flow of events which makes the static arrangements of the meta-men valueless and without permanence. The motion of things is such that our attempts to arrange and fix and determine are

[6] Ibid., p. 29.

The Auroras of Autumn   133

doomed to failure; the static suspension is forever jostled by the flowing events of being, and the artificial arrangement becomes a shambles and lies discarded in the end.

The nature of being is the unifying theme of the three long, meditative poems which are contained in *The Auroras of Autumn*. In the order of their inclusion in the volume, the poems are "Auroras of Autumn," "A Primitive Like an Orb," and "An Ordinary Evening in New Haven." All of them are loosely joined sets of short, musing poems in iambic pentameter, and all are difficult to explicate because of the private symbolism which Stevens employs and because the ordering of lines is not that of the conscious, rational mind, but rather that of free association of images and the processes of the subconscious mind.

The first poem of the series introduces us to the serpent of being, a creature who, like Shelley's west wind, is both creator and destroyer. The description of the creature is almost entirely in terms of oppositions—he is "height" and "base," "form" and "formlessness," "body" and "air." The wisdom of the serpent enables us for a moment to view him as "master of the maze . . ./ Relentlessly in possession of happiness" (CP, p. 411), but the wisdom and the poison of the serpent are one, for in an instant certainty is gone and we are filled with disbelief in the momentary vision and in the happiness of forms and images. The will to believe generates the will to disbelieve, and the rage of the mind for order is replaced by the mind's distrust of forms. Stevens, like Keats, learns that the fancy cannot cheat so well as she is famed to do.

The second section of "The Auroras of Autumn" contemplates the circumstances of man, aging, aware of the flow of time, and seeking some sort of rational order in the blowing sand and the ever-changing aurora borealis. The third, forth, and fifth sections of "Auroras" develop an extended metaphor in which the poet is the child of a highly impressionistic mother and father, a comparison which has been susceptible to a bewildering number of possible interpretations. The mother would seem to suggest the earth, whose face is "the purpose of the poem," who is gentle, but who has grown old. The father, measurer of "the velocities of change," and himself the origin of motion, seems to represent "the highest eye," the ultimate subjective force which is, of course, the creative imagination. This familial metaphor presents a poignant view of the aging poet, for, as the senses cool, the mother is seen as dissolving, as destroyed, as having "grown old." The father has deserted the family temporarily. He sits in space and in saying "yes to no" he says "farewell." Nonetheless, father and mother are reconciled in section five and jointly give a pageant featuring music and drama, a pageant which represents the poem.

Section six is the result of an imaginative transfer of the pageantry at the house of the mother and father in which the house and the guests become "a theatre floating through the clouds" and the drama of transformation is played out. Frank Doggett has linked this passage to others in Stevens which emphasize the ever-changing nature of being.

> The theater is filled with forms of life, like birds in flight, grouped, vanishing, clinging like a web. . . . The flying birds represent the procession of being, one of Stevens' many images for the ceaseless activity of life, such as the repeated movement of waves on a shore, the tumult of a festival, glistening shapes in a waltz, streams of marching men.[7]

The "single man," like the walker on the beach, views the flaring brilliance of the "Arctic effulgence" and is afraid, a fear with which the remainder of the poem must contend as best it can.

Section seven introduces a personified figure for the imagination which is very much like the figure of the father in sections three, four, and five. This figure, however, is

[7] Doggett, *Stevens' Poetry of Thought*, pp. 64–65.

larger, more universalized. In "Final Soliloquy of the Interior Paramour," Stevens muses, "We say God and the imagination are one" (CP, p. 254). That God figure is evoked in poem seven as the cause of all movement, a bodiless imagination that creates the world by conceiving it.

> Is there an imagination that sits enthroned
> As grim as it is benevolent, the just
> And the unjust, which in the midst of summer stops
>
> To imagine winter? When the leaves are dead,
> Does it take its place in the north and enfold itself,
> Goat-leaper, crystalled and luminous, sitting
>
> In the highest night? . . .
> (CP, p. 417)

The "goat leaper," a kind of Pan figure, is the desire of winter for its opposite, the force which in summer begins the descent to winter by the imagining of snow. Like the phenomenal world, the world of the imagination "must change," and even the godlike "goat leaper" has to "move to find/ What must unmake it and, at last, what can . . ." (CP, p. 418). Thus, poem seven concludes with the assertion that the life of the mind, like the life of the external world, moves in a cycle in which the winter of decreation is necessary if there is to be a corresponding season of creative blossomings.

Poems eight and nine suggest a time of innocence, a time which seems to exist more as a postulate of the mind than as a time having real existence. It exists "in the idea of it alone," a time in which man was "at the centre of the diamond" rather than hopelessly at the edge. The innocence, beauty, and unity of man and world is reminiscent of the Edenic *Harmonium* when "We were as Danes in Denmark all day long." Implicit in the remembrance of this "time of innocence"—and in *The Auroras of Autumn* such a time can be only a memory—are the suggestions of mortality which darkened many of the poems of *Harmonium* years before.

> Shall we be found hanging in the trees next spring?
> Of what disaster is this the imminence:
> Bare limbs, bare trees and a wind as sharp as salt?
>
> (CP, p. 419)

However, seen as a rendezvous with fate, the "great shadow" loses its terrors and becomes "Almost as part of innocence, almost,/ Almost as the tenderest and the truest part" (CP, p. 420).

The tenth and last poem of "Auroras of Autumn" is an attempt to summarize, to evaluate what has gone before. It is time to stand up, to make a statement about the relationship between man and his world. Stevens tries and rejects several descriptions of our condition. We are not, he decides, "An unhappy people in an unhappy world" (CP, p. 420), for such a view distorts by misusing the world as a mirror in which we think we see reality while seeing only our unhappy reflected selves. Nor, he asserts, are we "A happy people in a happy world" (CP, p. 420). No sensitive man, having once tasted life's bitter aspic, can accept the animated cartoon version as the truth of our being. Nor are we "A happy people in an unhappy world," for such a people could not have written poetry. There would be "nothing there to roll/ On the expressive tongue, the finding fang" (CP, p. 420). And we are a people who have produced poetry. Therefore, our condition is best summarized in the remaining alternative—we are "An unhappy people in a happy world" (CP, p. 420). As Donald Davie has pointed out, such a world view is not inconsistent with the traditional doctrine of the fortunate fall, in that our situation may be explained by the belief that "God requires in His Creation . . . an element of conflict to be reconciled, and hence a margin of freedom for man that leaves him capable of heroism." [8] However, Stevens, as always, chooses to create his own mythology, and the comparison with *Genesis* may be interesting, but it is not especially relevant. Instead of God, it is the "rabbi" who is addressed, the philosopher who has meditated on the human condition and seen that the movement which is life is the product of the tension created by living where we live. Man's struggle to be at one with this place that is "not our own," his desire to be at the center when he is doomed to be at the edge, his attempts at form and order in the flow of chaotic experience—from these interactings of the imagination with the world "solemnized in secretive syllables" the poem comes. And the poem which rolls our condition on the expressive tongue crystallizes, for the moment, what it is to be alive, captures, however briefly, the nature and tension of being.

Perhaps no poem in Stevens' collection makes a more explicit statement of the tragi-comic human condition than does "A Primitive Like an Orb." In a sense it demonstrates that all of the pain of our experience falls between "is" and "as," in the uncertain realm between objective reality and our imaginative metamorphoses of that reality. The flickerings between subject and object are the sum total of human experience, and our inability to make the two, "is" and "as," one is the source of our alienation from our home.

The first poem of "A Primitive Like an Orb" postulates the existence of "The essential poem at the centre of things," suggesting at first glance a brand of sloppy Platonism on Stevens' part. Later, however, we are to learn that the poem sheds a light which "is not a light apart, up-hill." Instead of being an ideal form, the "essential poem" is a poem which includes all poems and which derives its existence from them. Since any one individual poem is a partial record of human experience, one moment of being, the

[8] Davie, " 'The Auroras of Autumn,' " p. 177.

"essential poem" which contains all poems is the "supreme fiction," the perfect symbol for the truth of human life with nothing omitted, nothing snipped off to distort the truth.

The power of the individual poem to capture momentarily the sense of being opens to us the vision of the grand poem which would be complete and which would be as dynamic as being itself. As always, this sense of being is a fleeting, uncertain event.

> In the instant of speech,
> The breadth of an accelerando moves,
> Captives the being, widens—and was there.
>> (CP, p. 440)

In the instant of speech, the sound of the patient syllables of the individual poem proves the existence of the "central poem" to the satisfaction of "the clairvoyant men," "The lover, the believer, and the poet" (CP, p. 441).[9] Stevens assures us that the words of poets are "chosen out of their desire," in this case the desire to "see more than cool reason ever comprehends."

Poem five points to the function of "poet, believer, and lover." Each must free the world from its stale appearances, transform the "used-to tree" and the "used-to cloud" to new uses, new appearances. "It is," Stevens says, "As if the central poem became the world,/ And the world the central poem" (CP, p. 441). The central poem, as unimaginable, imagined perfect symbol for the world, for being, is the mirror image of the world, and, as he so frequently does, Stevens expresses the relationship between symbol and world in terms of a marriage. Each, he insists, must become

> the mate
> Of the other, as if summer was a spouse,
> Espoused each morning, each long afternoon,

[9] The grouping is reminiscent of the well-known speech of Duke Theseus in *A Midsummer Night's Dream*, in which Theseus affirms that "The lunatic, the lover, and the poet/ Are of imagination all compact" (V. i. 4–16).

And the mate of summer: her mirror and her look,
Her only place and person, a self of her
That speaks, denouncing separate selves, both one.

(CP, p. 441)

The central poem is capable of embracing the changing, varied flow of experience and pulling it into a unity, an "essential compact of the parts." The central poem is "The roundness that pulls tight the final ring . . ." (CP, p. 442). Sections eight, nine, ten, eleven, and twelve list the attributes of that poem, attributes which are, not surprisingly, those of the "supreme fiction." It must, we learn, be abstract, for the "giant" which Stevens uses to embody the central poem is "an abstraction given head" and has been created of "nothingness." It must bring pleasure, for it must be adorned with

> every prodigal, familiar fire,
> And unfamiliar escapades: whirroos
> And scintillant sizzlings such as children like,
> Vested in the serious folds of majesty,
> Moving around and behind, a following,
> A source of trumpeting seraphs in the eye,
> A source of pleasant outbursts on the ear.

(CP, p. 442)

And finally, it must change, as the final stanza makes perfectly clear. The individual artists are "eccentrics," only partial experiencers of being, and they can artistically reproduce only one part of the giant of the supreme fiction, "the skeleton of the ether." The concluding lines of the poem suggest that each work of art, each perception, and the giant are "ever changing, living in change" (CP, p. 443). It is the constant additions to the total of "letters, prophecies, perceptions," which make the giant alter. Each partial vision of the giant adds to the whole vision; each work of art adds to the tradition of the whole and alters the work of the future.

Although Stevens in "A Primitive Like an Orb" seems to think of the giant as the product of all the attempts to produce the symbol of truth, all of the attempts by all of the clairvoyant men, his own collected poems fall into much the same relationship to that symbol for the world. Each poem is a "clod of color," a blotch of blue or green or red or rose or white on the canvas, but the central poem is the poem of the whole, the total perception of the ever-altering moments recorded in his poetry, which views the blotches as a "composition," the final vision of the imagined giant.

The rapid flickering of oppositions, resulting in an effect much like the changing perceptions of an optical illusion, is nowhere more evident in Wallace Stevens' poetry than in "An Ordinary Evening in New Haven." In speaking of his purpose in writing the poem, Stevens announced that he wanted

> to try to get as close to the ordinary, the commonplace and the ugly as it is possible for a poet to get. . . . The object is of course to purge oneself of anything false. . . . This is not in any sense a turning away from the ideas of Credences of Summer: it is a development of those ideas.[10]

The key phrase here is "as it is possible for a poet to get." In "Credences of Summer" Stevens had explored the limits of reality—the hay fields near Oley, the gold sun in the white sky seen without metaphor—but he had learned that to announce the visible was to create something *more* than visible, that the creative effort acknowledges the human mind and the division of mind and physical universe. He had found also that when one explores the limits of reality,

> Things stop in that direction and since they stop
> The direction stops and we accept what is
> As good. . . .
> (CP, p. 374)

[10] Stevens, *Letters*, pp. 636–37.

When the direction stops, when one pursues reality far enough, he suddenly stumbles upon its opposite, perhaps in the realization that unadorned reality is an imagined concept, perhaps in the desire that one opposing value has to mingle with the other. The poet can only get so close to reality and then "a second giant kills the first" and the very emptiness of New Haven creates the conditions which demand imaginative additions.

> The plainness of plain things is savagery,
> As: the last plainness of a man who has fought
> Against illusion and was, in a great grinding
>
> Of growling teeth, and falls at night, snuffed out
> By the obese opiates of sleep. Plain men in plain towns
> Are not precise about the appeasement they need.
>
> They only know a savage assuagement cries
> With a savage voice; and in that cry they hear
> Themselves transposed, muted and comforted
>
> In a savage and subtle and simple harmony,
> A matching and mating of surprised accords,
> A responding to a diviner opposite.
>
> So lewd spring comes from winter's chastity.
> So, after summer, in the autumn air,
> Comes the cold volume of forgotten ghosts,
>
> But soothingly, with pleasant instruments,
> So that this cold, a children's tale of ice,
> Seems like a sheen of heat romanticized.
>
> (CP, pp. 467–68)

Poem six continues the discussion of the inter-related nature of phenomenal world and imagination. The phenomenal world, Stevens insists, is the basis of all poetry, the beginning from which men must build. The ever-changing nature of both is expressed in the following lines in which "Alpha" represents phenomenal reality, the beginning, and "Omega" represents the interpretation of that reality, the end of the process of experience: "Alpha continues to begin,/ Omega is refreshed at every end" (CP, p. 469). The phenomenal universe is forever beginning anew; the imagination is never satisfied with a final interpretation, but must be refreshed each time it comes to "an end."

Poems nine and ten are poems of desire and frustration, the desire of the poet to come to "The poem of pure reality, untouched/ By trope or deviation, straight to the word" (CP, p. 471), and the frustration of learning that, try as he will,

> The enigmatical
> Beauty of each beautiful enigma
>
> Becomes amassed in a total double-thing.
> We do not know what is real and what is not.
>
> (CP, p. 472)

Since imagination and external phenomena must be mixed, it follows that "The poem is the cry of its occasion,/ Part of the res itself and not about it" (CP, p. 473). Because what we say about an event is a part of the event, "said words of the world are the life of the world" (CP, p. 474). Therefore the poems of Wallace Stevens represent individual moments in which "the self/ The town, the weather, in a casual litter" have been given life by the syllables which say them.

Poem fourteen introduces the dramatic persona of Professor Eucalyptus of New Haven, who searches the commonplace objects which surround him in the hope of discovering an absolute reality which he may glorify as divine. The Professor's search constitutes a kind of *ars poetica* for Stevens, for it suggests the power of the imagination to apotheosize even the most inglorious of the objects of the world.

> It is a choice of the commodious adjective
> For what he sees, it comes in the end to that:

The description that makes it divinity, still speech
As it touches the point of reverberation—not grim
Reality but reality grimly seen.
                    (CP, p. 475)

To the Professor, a figure for the poet, the chaotic flow of reality, "The tink-tonk/ Of the rain in the spout" will not serve because it is "not yet well perceived." Only when it has merged with the language will it have been brought into perceptive focus; the poet can come only so near phenomenal reality, and this, of course, is Stevens' point.

These segments of "An Ordinary Evening in New Haven" are variations on a single theme—they explore the inadequacies of life lived totally in the commonplace world and the equal inadequacies of life lived only in an imaginative world. Either extreme, either opposite, will not suffice; they must be reconciled. The concluding poems of "Ordinary Evening," sections twenty-eight through thirty-one, are workings out of this merger.

If it should be true that reality exists
In the mind: . . .
        it follows that
Real and unreal are two in one.
                    (CP, p. 485)

And if the two are one, then "the theory of poetry is the theory of life," for "life" is neither imaginary nor coldly objective, but an interaction of the two. Poem twenty-nine is the symbolic working out of this thesis. The land of the lemon trees, exotic and beautiful, is visited by the prosaic mariners from "the land of the elm trees." Their reaction is poetic—they describe the lemon trees with such fluency as they have. " 'We are back once more in the land of the elm trees,/ But folded over, turned round' " (CP, p. 487). Their "dark-colored words" redescribe the lemon trees, making a change in them that is greater than any change of nature provided by falling light or shifting clouds. But in the same fashion, the encounter with the lemon trees has changed the dwellers in the land of the elm trees, for all experience produces an inner change. Thus, the poetic action has its reaction; the adjective gives and takes, and the soil and man's intelligence meet, mingle, and metamorphosize.

The last two poems return to the plight of the aging man and the search for reality, a rock to which to cling in the midst of flux.

It was something imagined that has been washed away.
A clearness has returned. It stands restored.

It is not an empty clearness, a bottomless sight.
It is a visibility of thought,
In which hundreds of eyes, in one mind, see at once.
(CP, p. 488)

To blood abstractions, give to meditation concrete shape and form, is, indeed, to create a "visibility of thought." And it is precisely a visibility of thought that Stevens' *Auroras of Autumn* have presented. For Stevens, the act of meditation is an act of self-definition in which one escapes from "the silence of summer" and from the temptation to give himself over to "a sad hanging on for remembrances." Having so escaped, the poet is freed by his meditations on the nature of experience to conclude that

It is not in the premise that reality
Is a solid. It may be a shade that traverses
A dust, a force that traverses a shade.
(CP, p. 489)

And, rid by long meditation of the concept of a fixed, solid reality, Stevens can affirm once more the flowing nature of life and the dependence of life on the attempts to produce "formulae/ Of statement" about it. Meditation, the meditation that produces poetry of thought, is a way of trying to give form to experience; however, like the note of the woman, written and then torn to bits, the forms must give

The Auroras of Autumn 145

way. They can suffice only as the cry of one occasion and cannot serve to present a reality which will not hold still for any form.

If the flow of life is to be symbolized, the symbol must take a form which constantly decreates itself and begins again, a form much like that of the rapidly moving succession of opposites which one encounters when Stevens' collection of poems is read as a single poem.

The Rock

The poetry of *The Rock* is supremely introspective. It is a poetry of private symbols growing out of seventy-five years of personal associations. The poems of *The Rock* look backward and forward at the same time, and, while seeking the reality of the present moment, look inward to the workings of the mind as if reality were to be found there. *The Rock* is a poetry of acceptance, not only of the fact of death, but also of the impossibility of ever isolating in pure form either the subjective world or the objective world toward which Stevens had alternately groped through earlier volumes. *The Rock* represents one last attempt to capture being in artistic form, and Stevens makes an effort to present the alternation of reality and fiction in such a way as to capture the sense of flowing motion which our minds, in their interaction with the phenomenal universe, know as life.

Ironically, in terms of technique, Stevens' last works in *The Collected Poems* are more dramatic than are the poems of most of the other volumes after *Harmonium*. The tone of the last volume is, as one would expect, markedly different from that of the first, but, as Joseph Riddel has observed, "Preparing for his farewell, Stevens seems to come back to the intense love of the physical world that was his starting point." [1] *The Rock* has its dramatic characters—Mr. Homberg, Ulysses and Penelope, Ariel, the old philosopher who is dying in Rome—and the characters are placed upon appropriate stages and given lines to speak. All of the voices, however, sound much alike, and many of the figures are not even intended to serve as effectual masks. Where Stevens once used the dramatic persona to probe the possible extremes of mind and soil, he now speaks from behind the mask to maintain a degree of impersonality in facing up to death as a basic condition of life.

The land which these poet-figures inhabit is beautiful, in its way perhaps more beautiful than that of *Harmonium,* but the beauty of *The Rock* is the bare, sad beauty of late autumn, not the colorful, vibrant beauty of spring in Eden. There is motion, as motion was present in the scene in *Harmonium,* but it is a motion of things flowing away—of wood-smoke blown above the trees, of birds flying across empty fields, of departing human beings and boats and sunlight, of the river that flows nowhere, the tracks in the snow of March which shift and change as the sun melts them.

The drowsy sense of meditation, of a mind turning problems over on the edge of sleep, is established with the very first poem of *The Rock.*

> The two worlds are asleep, are sleeping, now.
> A dumb sense possesses them in a kind of solemnity.
>
> The self and the earth— . . .
>
> The redness of your reddish chestnut trees,
> The river motion, the drowsy motion of the river R.
>
> (CP, p. 501)

Neither imagination nor earth has much vitality; a kind of stupor has settled over both. What is left is the drowsy questioning of "The Irish Cliffs of Moher." "Who is my

[1] Riddel, *Clairvoyant Eye,* p. 243.

father in this world," asks Stevens, a question which is but another version of that "Mother, my mother, who are you," of the "drowsy, infant" old men in "Questions Are Remarks." In the appropriately titled "Long and Sluggish Lines," Stevens seemingly addresses himself when he says, "You were not born yet when the trees were crystal/ Nor are you now, in this wakefulness inside a sleep" (CP, p. 522). This sleepy state seems to me to be a figure for the mind's inwardness, a "wakefulness," but a wakefulness "inside a sleep." The images that float across the pages come from within the self; as in one's dreams, the characters who speak and act are aspects of one's own concerns, desires, and fears. Having descended into these dreamlike meditative depths, the consciousness can go no farther in that direction, and Stevens, realizing this limitation, ends his *Collected Poems* with "Not Ideas about the Thing but the Thing Itself," a poem which is a call from outside the mind, a "scrawny cry" uttered by the external world.

> At the earliest ending of winter,
> In March, a scrawny cry from outside
> Seemed like a sound in his mind.
>
> (CP, p. 534)

Everything about the concluding poem of Stevens' collection cries out "beginning." It is spring, a spring so new that it is still "the earliest ending of winter." It is morning, and so early morning that the time is "daylight or before." The bird cry is the first, for this bird precedes all others as a harbinger of new life. At first the cry seems "a sound in his mind," for the mind has turned in upon itself for so long that it hears only itself in a dialog like that of ventriloquist and dummy. And yet,

> It was not from the vast ventriloquism
> Of sleep's faded papier-mâché . . .
> The sun was coming from outside.
>
> (CP, p. 534)

The cry punctures the papier-mâché of sleep to draw the sleeper back to the natural world, the phenomenal world. The faded sun, that "battered panache," once again becomes the "colossal sun," a sun that has all but disappeared from Stevens' work since *Harmonium*, and, although it is "Still far away," the poet breathes deeply again and sets out once more to follow the sun. As one would expect, Stevens' symbol for the process of life is open-ended, for being itself is continuous motion and has no end.

The tensions of *The Rock* are familiar. Stevens still moves from the real to the imagined, from the external world to the internal world, but now the movement is much more rapid, and the tension is meant to be a poetic representation of the truth of our being. Neither pure imagined land nor pure objective land exists for us, but the truth of our being consists of a constant oscillation between those poles, even though the poles have existence only as necessary postulates of the mind. Stevens' task as artist is to create somehow a symbol which will be accurate to the facts of our condition, a poem which will capture the rapid and endless flow of our experience from mind to object, from object to mind. The poems of *The Rock* are poems of a mind meditating on what it is to be, to experience life, and the mind concludes that life is neither object nor subject but the constant movement between the two. That movement, so rapid that it blurs into the illusion of a solid object, is our present moment, the moment that represents all the being and life that exist anywhere.[2]

Stevens tries to represent this flux in a variety of ways. The continuity of experience is emphasized most obviously and most simply by the retrospective mood of the volume and by the continued use of poetic images which have originated in earlier volumes. The image of the rock was

[2] In his essay "Wallace Stevens: The Last Lessons of the Master" (pp. 126–27) Roy Harvey Pearce has spoken of these movements and their consequences for Stevens in his later work.

first used in *Ideas of Order* in the poem entitled "How to Live. What to Do." The history of the image in Stevens' work has been carefully traced by Ralph J. Mills, Jr., in an article called "Wallace Stevens: The Image of the Rock." Moreover, the familiar Stevens images for the imagination, for reality, for being, are all present in *The Rock*—the moon and the earth and the sun; red and turquoise and blue and green; the house and the candle and the river. Each image, each time it is used, carries with it the history of all of Stevens' uses of that image through the years and is altered and heightened by the clouds of associations which it trails. Since each image occurs in a new context each time it appears, its meaning becomes a product of the interaction of the total past and the immediate present, a relationship much like that of all human experience in which each moment receives meaning from the past and at the same time alters the meaning of all that has come before by adding to it.

The retrospective mood and tone of the volume is so pervasive as scarcely to need mention, but such poems as "The Planet on the Table" and "The Rock" and "Long and Sluggish Lines" are so linked by memory to the past that they can hardly be read in isolation. They are Wallace Stevens at "so much more than seventy," and could be the poems of no one else. They are joined to his special and particular past by theme, by image, and by allusion; they must be taken as Stevens intended them—as parts of the whole, a pulling tight of the final ring. As the products of immense repetitions, these poems of *The Rock* are a stage in a process of evolution; they are not spontaneous creations out of emptiness such as the Herr Gott was once imagined to have wrought for reasons known only to himself.

The sense of movement, however, is most effectively and most significantly presented in those poems which in one way or another present the objective view of the world and the subjective view of the world so superimposed upon each other that we are aware of the flickering dizziness caused by the rapid changes from "is" to "as" and back again. One of the most experimental of these poems is the one called "The Hermitage at the Center." The poem is a *tour de force*—five three-line stanzas in which the first lines of each stanza form a kind of poem within a poem.

> The leaves on the macadam make a noise—
> How soft the grass on which the desired
> Reclines in the temperature of heaven—
>
> Like tales that were told the day before yesterday—
> Sleek in a natural nakedness,
> She attends the tintinnabula—
>
> And the wind sways like a great thing tottering—
> Of birds called up by more than the sun,
> Birds of more wit, that substitute—
>
> Which suddenly is all dissolved and gone—
> Their intelligible twittering
> For unintelligible thought.
>
> And yet this end and this beginning are one,
> And one last look at the ducks is a look
> At lucent children round her in a ring.
>
> (CP, pp. 505–506)

The complete sentence which the first lines of the stanzas make up is an autumnal sentence of dissolution, mutability, and "totterings." The remaining lines, on the other hand, present a picture of lushness, warmth, gay birds, and nakedness. In short, we have Stevens' winter mood and his summer mood juxtaposed, a world of barren and sombre falling leaves and a world of imagined queens and of birds whose songs are "intelligible." "The desired" would seem to be another of Stevens' figures for the imagination, a midsummer, naked, fictive queen whose power transforms the ducks into "lucent children" in an ordered and perfect "ring."

The "hermitage" that is at "the center" does not seem to be at the center of the ring of children—one does not refer to a hermitage as "she"—but rather appears to be at some center between the two worlds, a center which composes both imagination and reality so that the poet can affirm that "this end and this beginning are one." The poem is two poems, each intelligible in its own right, but the two poems become one in the last stanza. The summer and the winter vision merge into a unified whole in which end and beginning, the aged man and the children, are joined in the figure of the ring, yet each maintains its separate identity.

Something of the same double vision may be seen in "To an Old Philosopher in Rome," Stevens' tribute to George Santayana, which becomes, by extension, a tribute to all men whose lives are examples of the powers of the intelligence. The world of the imagination and the world of reality are both present, flickering in the atmosphere of the room in which the old philosopher is dying. There is a mixture of the physical and the symbolic, the particular and the abstract, the "figures in the street" and "the figures of heaven." These two dimensions are designated as "Rome," the actual city of nuns, books, and chairs, and as "that more merciful Rome/ Beyond," the realm of "the celestial possible" (CP, pp. 508–11). The flame of an actual candle becomes the fires of heaven and the mutterings of newsboys become "another murmuring," more meaningful, more divine. For the moment, Santayana is both citizen of heaven and citizen of Rome. The tension between the natural desire to cling as long as possible to the life of the actual city and the desire of the spirit "To join a hovering excellence" makes the poem one of the finest that Stevens ever wrote. It is this tension, effectively maintained, which enables us, like Santayana and like Stevens himself, to live "in two worlds" at the same time, or, more accurately, at so nearly the same time that we share the heightened awareness of "being" which is so acutely present in the death room. The sense of this awareness is the final reward of the meditative life which leads to the ultimate vision.

> It is a kind of total grandeur at the end,
> With every visible thing enlarged and yet
> No more than a bed, a chair and moving nuns,
> The immensest theatre, the pillared porch,
> The book and candle in your ambered room . . .
>
> (CP, p. 510)

Santayana, like Stevens, watches the commonplace transformed, apotheosized by the imagination, and yet the transformation leaves the commonplace things no more than themselves, still very much of this earth, this time.

The most vital words of the final lines of the poem seem to me to be the words "As if."

> He stops upon this threshold,
> As if the design of all his words takes form
> And frame from thinking and is realized
>
> (CP, p. 511)

Frank Doggett has suggested that the philosophic structure of Santayana's life is "to be left as a building or a city may be left, standing there for other inhabitants," [3] but I suspect that Stevens knows only too well that the recognition of "form" and "frame" is at best the possibility of a moment, perhaps only of a moment of passage, a brief vision of a structure glimpsed while standing on a threshold; Santayana cannot remain in the doorway, and the structure and form and design of the edifice he has erected will begin to tremble in the instant that he steps over the threshold.

One such tumbled edifice is St. Armorer's Church, once "an immense success" as the perfect symbol for its age, but now a decaying ruin to be viewed by men of the twentieth century "from the outside" only.

> St. Armorer's was once an immense success.
> It rose loftily and stood massively; and to lie

[3] Doggett, *Stevens' Poetry of Thought*, p. 124.

In its church-yard, in the province of St. Armorer's,
Fixed one for good in geranium-colored day.

(CP, p. 529)

The imagery is entirely static. The church "stood mas-
sively," and to be buried in its province was to be "Fixed"
forever in the hope of heaven.

Now, however, "A sumac grows/ On the altar, growing
toward the lights, inside" (CP, p. 529). The living tree is a
more modern symbol, a familiar romantic symbol for organic growth, change, and development. The tree is not
fixed and dead, and its arching branches form a living
"chapel," a "yes" among "cindery noes."

> St. Armorer's has nothing of this present,
> This *vif*, this dizzle-dazzle of being new
> And of becoming, for which the chapel spreads out
> Its arches in its vivid element,
>
> In the air of newness of that element,
> In an air of freshness, clearness, greenness, blueness,
> That which is always beginning because it is part
> Of that which is always beginning, over and over.

(CP, p. 530)

The tree and the church are tensively opposed symbols, the
one living, and, because it is living, continuously in process;
and the other a crumbling relic because it was never alive,
but only static, perfect, and immense. As always in Stevens'
work, "That which is always beginning" succeeds while that
which is complete and fixed and perfect is doomed to fail.

The lovely poem called "The World as Meditation" is one
in which imagination and phenomenal "reality," mind and
world, are figures in an endless process which never
achieves stasis, but which never ceases to struggle toward
that unattainable goal. The poem is an excellent example of
the dramatic form that Stevens employs in *The Rock*. There
is a setting, a character, and a situation that leads to a kind
of action, but the action is almost entirely the meditative

act of Penelope, and Penelope herself is much more a symbol than she is flesh and blood woman. As might be expected, Penelope, imaginative, passive, and feminine, represents the active mind, and the absent Ulysses, that "interminable adventurer," represents that world of physical phenomena from which we are hopelessly separated, a world which we can never experience except as it comes to us filtered through the senses and tainted by the mind.

Ulysses and Penelope are not to be united. Yet, from her "barbarous strength" and from her desire for the "Someone" or something "out there" in the phenomenal world is derived a force similar to that which mends the trees, awakens the world, and washes away the winter. Her strength is creative; her desire for unadorned reality, for companionship with "the thing itself," is the force which continually remakes the world for the man of imagination. In the composition of her self, in the imagining of a self for Ulysses as companion, Penelope's meditation becomes in itself a good; it is not necessary that their "deep-founded sheltering" ever actually house them. Indeed, it is impossible that it should ever do so, for being as we experience it is to be found neither in unreachable earth itself, nor in Penelope's meditations, nor, for that matter, in the two together. Being exists only in the forces which attract those opposites which can never quite meet. As J. Hillis Miller puts it, "Man's inability to see being as being causes the poet to say of it: 'It is and it/ Is not and, therefore, is' [CP, p. 440]," [4] and, similarly, out of Penelope's meditation comes the truth that "It was Ulysses and it was not" (CP, p. 521). The imagination encounters the world, but never the undistorted world. The moment of intersection is always a shade too brief, a matter of "was" rather than of "is," a presence which the eye is never quick enough to catch. Life is composed of a series of such encounters, and as each passes, nothing

[4] Miller, "Wallace Stevens' Poetry of Being," p. 158.

remains of the moment of being but what the poet says of it and his faithfulness to what it might have been, to what the next moment might become. Thus, Penelope, like a true poet,

> would talk a little to herself as she
> combed her hair,
> Repeating his name with its patient syllables,
> Never forgetting him that kept coming
> constantly so near.
> (CP, p. 521)

The poignancy of this our condition is expressed by Stevens in "Vacancy in the Park," a brief poem in which a series of images represents the present moment which is continually slipping away into the past.

> March . . . Someone has walked across the snow,
> Someone looking for he knows not what.
>
> It is like a boat that has pulled away
> From a shore at night and disappeared.
>
> It is like a guitar left on a table
> By a woman, who has forgotten it.
> (CP, p. 511)

The snow of March will soon melt, obliterating the last trace of the seeker of being. Perhaps the tracks he has left are like poems, a record of the search he made, and, if so, one is reminded of Stevens' affirmation in "The Planet on the Table" that "It was not important" that his poems should "survive" (CP, p. 532). Of being one can say only that something *was* there, but the winds continue to blow and the present moment flows into the past, which can only be a vacancy, an emptiness, because all time and all being is eternally present. Thus, even before April becomes May, the snows of March are but a stale metaphor for irretrievable time; the ship will not return; the woman will not reclaim the guitar; the feeling of the man who comes to see the "certain house" cannot be determined and labeled.

Several of the poems of *The Rock* are investigations of the world by a man who feels that he has lost something of the shaping power of the imagination; and, for Stevens, to come to an "end of the imagination" would be to come to an end of life itself. In "The Plain Sense of Things," for example, the phenomenal world is perceived at its shabbiest, with the slightest possible adornment. "The greenhouse never so badly needed paint," Stevens writes, and one sees that the house of blank, colorless glass is a house now badly in need of the gildings of the imagination. However, one can advance only so far in the direction of either imagined land or of land totally without imagination before discovering the futility of the journey. And, at more than seventy, Stevens knows well the impossibility of finding a resting place along the way. Although he can affirm that "It is as if/ We had come to an end of the imagination" (CP, p. 502), Stevens recognizes the importance of the qualifying "as if." There is no end to our imaginings, no resting in "the plain sense of things." Despite the static imagery and the absence of any sense of movement in pond or leaves, the mind is still moving, and the pathos of the desolate scene is, in part, in the hard *necessity* in the phrase "had to be imagined" (CP, p. 503). The final vision, reality unveiled, has itself to be imagined, for we cannot free ourselves from our involuntary destiny to shape the world we inhabit. We come to the point of death as fact, to the "blank cold" for which there is no coloring, and discover that even the blankness itself demonstrates that there *is* no end of the imagination, but that the mind touches even that emptiness. In fact, the imagination chooses the adjectives it denies, even in "The Plain Sense of Things." It chooses *blank, like dirty glass, waste,* and *lessened.*

"Long and Sluggish Lines" begins with the same sense of blankness, with the wintry emptiness of the February trees and the poignancy of the wood-smoke being whirled away beyond the trees; however, this poem also embodies a sense of double vision, for the tragedy has its comic side. The barren trees are in an uproar "because an opposite, a contradiction,/ Has enraged them . . ." (CP, p. 522).

> What opposite? Could it be that yellow patch, the side
> Of a house, that makes one think the house is laughing;
>
> Or these—escent—issant pre-personae: first fly,
> A comic infanta among the tragic drapings,
>
> Babyishness of forsythia, a snatch of belief
> The spook and makings of the nude magnolia?
> (CP, p. 522)

Here is a tension between poetry of flat, descriptive statement—"Wood-smoke rises through trees, is caught in an upper flow/ Of air and whirled away"—and the poetry of the imagination in which the yellow patch of the side of the house personifies the house and gives it a life of its own. Out of the barrenness comes the demand of the opposite for recognition, and the leafless trees cannot talk down the laughing house and the intimations of new life any more than the flow of being can be arrested. As in "The World as Meditation," the force of the poetic imagination is likened to the force which drives the seasons forward so relentlessly. The mind can never be satisfied, never, and bare winter must give way to spring.

Much the same movement takes place in "Lebensweisheitspielerei." Once again, the poem begins with a sense of diminishing light, and with it, the sense that all things are diminished.

> Weaker and weaker, the sunlight falls
> In the afternoon. The proud and the strong
> Have departed.
> (CP, p. 504)

Those who are left, "the unaccomplished,/ The finally human," remind one of old King Lear's "unaccommodated man," and, as representatives of the thing itself, these survivors may be yet another of Stevens' figures for unadorned reality. However,

> Little by little, the poverty
> Of autumnal space becomes
> A look, a few words spoken.
> (CP, p. 505)

As the words are spoken, each survivor is somewhat transformed, and each becomes shabbily radiant with "the stale grandeur of annihilation." There is no thing itself. The mind, beholding in others that yellow-leaved time of year, discovers itself "touched" and bestows upon the aged a kind of value and worth that is, perhaps, not their own, that is, perhaps, akin to love.

The title poem of Stevens' final volume is one of his most successful meditations on the nature of being and of the relationship of poetry to it. The turquoise rock is thought by various critics to represent various things, but beneath the apparent disagreements all of the critical "rocks" are fundamentally much alike. The rock is the symbol for being, a figure for reality, provided that one realizes that *reality* as used here is always *someone's* reality and always includes the poetry that the self makes in encountering the physical universe. Ralph J. Mills, Jr., succeeds in defining the rock effectively by substituting a poetic comparison of his own for the rock itself.

> Perhaps we might best think of a set of mirrors (imagination and reality) facing each other, which in-between themselves make a habitable world out of their blending reflections. The rock is the space of that world, and the wholeness it comes to imply in this late poetry contains sacramental meanings for Stevens.[5]

[5] Mills, "Wallace Stevens: The Image of the Rock," p. 107.

Of course, this "habitable world" in which the images of mind and world merge is the only dwelling place we have, the present moment. Doggett reinforces this notion by pointing out that "Schopenhauer uses the rock to indicate enduring existence in the midst of flux: 'time is like an unceasing stream, and the present a rock on which the stream breaks itself, but does not carry away with it.'" Doggett then remarks that "For Stevens the image has many possibilities, for as is true of the word *reality*, the image of the rock comprises everything that exists." [6] True enough, although one must remember that all being, the reality in which man lives, exists only and always in the present. Nothing else has existence but this permanence, this rock from which the flow of experience falls away into thought and memory. Thus, ironically enough, the flickering opposites of mind and world, oscillating with enough rapidity, blend together and form a solid image. The present is both eternal and ephemeral; "The present is always beginning over and over because it has no sooner begun than it has gone all the way to the end, and has moved so rapidly that 'this end and this beginning are one' [CP, p. 509]." [7]

The poem itself examines this paradox of merged origin and end on a number of levels. The title of the opening section, "*Seventy Years Later*," suggests a stage direction, a way of informing an audience that much time has elapsed between scenes, though no action has been shown to represent the intervening years. Stage time is no process; the curtain falls, years pass in darkness, the curtain rises and it is "seventy years later." The aged poet finds himself regarding the young Wallace Stevens with a sense of astonished disbelief. That the two should be somehow connected, should bear the same name, is beyond credence. Yet, the word *later* implies a connection, however tenuous, with

[6] Doggett, "*Stevens' Poetry of Thought*, pp. 195, 196.
[7] Miller, "Wallace Stevens' Poetry of Being," p. 151.

something that has gone before. The passing of time is being measured against an event that took place seventy years before.

Looking back over seventy years, Stevens once more uses the house as a symbol of the shell of a discarded idea, a way of looking at the world. The houses, perhaps the poems of an earlier time, "still stand,/ Though they are rigid in rigid emptiness" (CP, p. 525). It is the rigidity of the house which makes Stevens continually bid it farewell, for no permanent structure can keep pace with life.

Even our shadows, their shadows, no longer remain. . . .
They never were . . . The sounds of the guitar

Were not and are not. Absurd. The words spoken
Were not and are not. It is not to be believed.
                                        (CP, p. 525)

Shadows in Stevens' work are often products of the imagination, and at this point Stevens cannot even speak of his imaginative creations of the past as "our" shadows. The shadows are, he corrects himself, "their shadows." Stevens seems to regard the self at seventy as so many separate selves, a composite of all of the selves he has been and all he is becoming even as he speaks. His sense of separation from the past is such that he regards his earlier fictions as belonging to quite another man. Thus, the sounds of the (blue) guitar are the poems of someone else, and they are no longer audible to the seventy-year-old ear. And yet, as Riddel notes, this severance from the past is a creative act, an affirmation of the force of life which must continually destroy in order to raise up.[8]

Although Ralph J. Mills, Jr., sees the "embrace between one desperate clod/ And another" of the first section of "The Rock" as Stevens' claim "that love and human relationships,

---

[8] Riddel, *Clairvoyant Eye*, p. 249.

at this remove in time, are grotesque," [9] I do not believe the context of the embrace will support this interpretation. Stevens has been talking of his past, specifically of the poems which mark that past. The guitar, the houses, the shadows have all been representations of ideas, states of mind, and poems which have been abandoned so completely that it is as if they never were his at all. The next lines, the meeting of "clods" at the "field's edge," seem to me to be a continuation of the theme of moments of poetic felicity that are somehow cut off from his present state. The meeting might be that of two human beings, but might more consistently be that union of imagination and reality, that noon embrace that Stevens sang of in "Notes toward a Supreme Fiction." The great captain and the maiden Bawda married at noon on the midday of the year, and in "What We See Is What We Think" twelve was the hour at which green was greenest and blue bluest, "The imprescriptible zenith, free of harangue" (CP, p. 459). The meeting is at the edge of "the field" of the phenomenal world, neither in the field nor out of it, but always and hopelessly "at the edge." The earth is a "clod," but so is, in another and more ironic sense, the mind, and the embrace of the two as Stevens has presented it in "Notes" and elsewhere is an assertion of what it is to be human.

The rock is equated with "nothingness," an appropriate equation for a non-substantive *relationship*, a non-material, non-mental something "less tangible than the finest mist." [10] Yet one's desire to fix the nothingness that is our being is such that the force of will alone can produce "green leaves" and "lilacs" to cover the rock.

> The blooming and the musk
> Were being alive, an incessant being alive,
> A particular of being, that gross universe.
>> (CP, p. 526)

[9] Mills, "Wallace Stevens: The Image of the Rock," p. 106.
[10] Miller, "Wallace Stevens' Poetry of Being," p. 157.

To cover the rock with leaves is to make it visible, to cover its cold nothingness and hence to distort even while making beautiful. The will makes the rock over, but the blossoms of green are no longer sufficient for Stevens at seventy-five. Section II of "The Rock" introduces a new approach to being, a way of making meanings of the rock and in those meanings finding a health, a salvation.

> It is not enough to cover the rock with leaves.
> We must be cured of it by a cure of the ground
> Or a cure of ourselves, that is equal to a cure
>
> Of the ground, a cure beyond forgetfulness.
>
> (CP, p. 526)

In this passage *the ground* and *ourselves* are, I believe, simply new terms for *the soil* and *the intelligence* of *Harmonium*. The *Or* which opens line three must not be read as suggesting a choice, as an *either/or*. In the context of Stevens' struggles and failures to reach "the ground" in pure form, the *Or* of line three must be read as introducing a correction to what has come before. It is as if the line read, "Or, more accurately, a cure of ourselves that is equal to a cure/ Of the ground." This "cure" then, would be a blending once again of self and soil, an act of the mind which might serve as an accurate symbol for the world and thus be "equal to" a "cure of the ground." Such an act of the mind would be "the poem as icon," a new term for the "supreme fiction." At so much more than seventy, Stevens asserts that it is "not enough to cover the rock with leaves," and yet he knows, too, that

> the leaves, if they broke into bud,
> If they broke into bloom, if they bore fruit,
>
> And if we ate the incipient colorings
> Of their fresh culls might be a cure of the ground.
>
> (CP, p. 526)

The poem is not the world, is not being itself. It is not enough to cure us, and yet paradoxically the poem alone might be that "cure beyond forgetfulness" for lack of which we are dying. The poem as icon "makes meanings of the rock," resolves the chaos and whirl that is life, and so preserves us against the barrenness of being.

Being, and the rock is being, is neither self nor world, and since it is neither, but rather a flickering between them, it is nothing. The poem is both self and world given form and so juxtaposed that the icon becomes the outward and visible manifestation of that which cannot be made visible except in the form of an icon.

Accordingly, Mills describes the rock as having "sacramental meanings for Stevens. These meanings are bodied forth in the images of the leaves to suggest a kind of sanctification." [11] The rock-divinity which Stevens worships is being itself, life, and the idol before which he kneels is the work of art which makes meaning of the barrenness of being. The poem, the meaning the artist gives to being, transforms the world and the self at once; in bringing meaning and order to the flow of things, the poet has brought about a fictive formulation which corresponds to the Christian formulation in which he can no longer believe. Like that Christian myth, the poem as icon is a human creation which enables man to endure the condition in which he finds himself. For Stevens, the poem is an improvement because it disavows rigidified doctrine and creed and is, instead, "of such mixed motion" that it partakes of the changing nature of being. The earlier myth will not serve in a universe which is conceived to be dynamic, living in change and motion. The poem can cure us in the sense that it is capable of redeeming us from that fall which forever left us aliens in the only home we have. As Mills points out, one of Stevens' *Adagia* reads, "After one has

[11] Mills, "Wallace Stevens: The Image of the Rock," p. 107.

abandoned a belief in god, poetry is that essence which takes its place as life's redemption [OP, p. 158]." [12]

The third section of "The Rock," *Forms of the Rock in a Night-Hymn,* is a meditation upon the rock as both origin and end of what it is to be human. In a sense, section III is an illustration, an icon in which self and world attain such union as is possible. Through man's eye, Stevens says, the rock becomes "turquoise," the blue-green color which, being neither blue nor green, partakes of both. The rock, as a figure for being, "is the habitation of the whole," and, since being, the present and only moment, is forever in motion, it is "point A/ In a perspective that begins again/ At B" (CP, p. 528). The rock is

> The starting point of the human and the end,
> That in which space itself is contained, the gate
> To the enclosure, day, the things illumined
>
> By day, night and that which night illumines,
> Night and its midnight-minting fragrances,
> Night's hymn of the rock, as in a vivid sleep.
>
> (CP, p. 528)

The reconciliation of beginning and ending, day and night, enclosure and gate to the enclosure, gives a sense of the flickering of moments as perspective shifts from point A to point B. Mills has said of these closing stanzas of "The Rock" that they "draw together the circle of existence as Stevens envisages its certainty, a circle supported by the prevailing substance of the physical world and by the poem played upon that reality throughout a lifetime—a poem that remains after death." [13]

In a sense, then, the poem "Of such mixed motion and such imagery" that it transforms the barren rock into the wholeness of "a thousand things" is Stevens' answer to the problem posed by the monocled uncle—what becomes of

[12] Ibid., p. 108.
[13] Ibid., p. 109.

the balding amorist? The fact of death and decay is best confronted by a fiction which orders and gives meaning to the human condition. Over and over, in the *Adagia,* in the *Letters,* in the final poetry, we come to the same truth: "The final belief is to believe in a fiction, which you know to be a fiction, there being nothing else. The exquisite truth is to know that it is a fiction and that you believe in it willingly" (OP, p. 163).

In the "Final Soliloquy of the Interior Paramour," a particularly eschatological poem, we find that the thought in which "we collect ourselves" is that "The world imagined is the ultimate good" (CP, p. 524). Our fiction, our imagined meaning with which we cover the rock, is both a unifying force and a protection, a "single shawl" which we wrap around ourselves against the cold. It is, "since we are poor, a warmth/ A light, a power, the miraculous influence" (CP, p. 524). Our poverty, a term which aptly describes the condition of the homeless, is in the barrenness of the rock. Yet, within one fiction, the poem which makes the rock bring forth flowers, we find "an order, a whole, a knowledge." And out of this knowledge we can find that, for Stevens at least, "God and the imagination are one."

Afterword

To say that any serious artist must try to define and present reality is, perhaps, only to restate the Morse Peckham pronouncement with which I began this study: "The artist is the man who creates a symbol of the truth." Stevens, like most of us, begins with the assumption that "the real" is what is "out there" in the phenomenal universe, that kickable, tastable, visible, smellable "things" are "reality," and that any imaginative colorings that man adds to those "things" somehow makes them less "real." In fact, when using the term "reality" casually, in notes not meant to be published, in letters, Stevens almost always means the phenomenal, objective world. Unlike most of us, however, Stevens has his "Hoon moods," moments in which he flirts with the idea that "man is the intelligence of his soil," the creator of the world he lives in. At any rate, in the early poetry Stevens speaks of the struggle between "reality" and the imagination and obviously means the world of "things" to be "reality." Crispin, after all, begins with Hoon's world view, but comes to the notion that "man's soil is his intelligence," and such is generally the notion supported by *Harmonium*. Nonetheless, the relationship between object and subject is of major concern to Stevens from the beginning, and his meditations on that relationship in one way and another are what the *Collected Poems* are all about.

The relationship is at first viewed as a tension, a conflict in which the poet finds himself first on one side, and then on the other. The various pairings of figures for mind and soil—blue and green, clouds and sea, queens and soldiers, moon and sun—appear in opposition time after time, and Stevens is equally charmed by sun and moon. The conflict is presented for the most part in dramatic form; there are a setting, characters, action. And as the drama continues Stevens comes more and more to realize that Mrs. Uruguay's ultimate, unfalsified reality is itself an imaginative concept. To "see" the world without the tintings of the mind would be just another tinting of the mind, another fiction. And since all fictions rely on the phenomenal world for their origin and substance, neither purely imaginative world nor purely objective world can be a possibility.

The dramatic form of the early poetry increasingly gives way to meditation upon the nature of the dramatic conflict. In a sense, Stevens turns drama critic and examines the assumptions, limitations, presuppositions, and texture of the dramatic form he has produced and directed. He becomes more and more prone to write about the nature of the relationship between mind and soil, less and less prone to see the two as diametrically opposed or as in conflict only. The various figures for mind and objective world never completely drop out of Stevens' poetry, but in his later work he treats the figures more and more like counters in a game, as convenient shorthand forms for the abstractions they embody, and less and less like concrete entities with actual settings.

The counters and abstractions are manipulated much more rapidly than were Crispin and Hoon, Florida and New Jersey, and Mrs. Uruguay and the nameless rider who rides past her. They grow into one another, marry, merge, appear and disappear, separate and come together again in a bewildering dance at bewildering speed. Finally, as pointed out in my final chapter, the idea of the phenomenal world and the idea of the imagined land oscillate so rapidly that they form the illusion of a solid image out of the very rapidity of their movement. The image is, of course, the rock. That image becomes for Stevens the figure for reality, or the truth of human experience, and it is fitting that his final vision, his last poems, should be entitled simply "The Rock." Ironically, the image that would seem most stable, most certain, most fixed, turns out to be in point of fact totally illusory, for the rock exists only in change, motion, process. Reality, when Stevens finally comes to it, is dynamic, an ever-shifting relationship between phenomenal world and imagination. It is interesting to note how Stevens' dynamic rock is consistent with the view of the universe which physicists now assure us is the "true" one. Modern science tells us that all objects are in reality only space, that even the smallest electrical particle is now assumed to be only a tiny bit of whirling space, inexplicably "thrown into dervish-like vortex, emanating energies as by-products whose illusory forms (waves, electrical impulses) we interpret as 'matter' through our limited perceptions." [1] Stevens' rock is also an illusory form, a movement between two poles which themselves exist only as necessary postulates of the mind, a movement so rapid that there appears to be no motion at all —much as we are assured that we should be standing still if we were "travelling" at the speed of light.

The rock is a mystery, then, a paradox. It exists neither in the imagination nor in the phenomenal world—and there is nowhere else to exist but in the imagination or the phenomenal world. And yet it is more real than either mind or world, for the truth of human experience lies in neither, but in the relationship—the dynamic relationship—be-

[1] Richard Lippold, "Illusion as Structure," pp. 214–27.

tween the two. And so the truth of the rock is the truth of human experience.

How can we live with the shapeless, barren uncertainties of motion, of "the rock of reality"? In the dissertation on the nature of the rock which is the title poem of the last section of *The Collected Poems,* Stevens answers that question.

> In this plenty, the poem makes meanings of the rock,
> Of such mixed motion and such imagery
> That its barrenness becomes a thousand things

> And so exists no more. This is the cure
> Of leaves and of the ground and of ourselves.
> (CP, p. 527)

The rock is what there is—motion, relationship, change—and if the poem is to be true to "what there is," it must mirror those conditions, must make meanings of "mixed motion" and beflower the barren rock with "a thousand things." The poem must be dynamic because reality is dynamic, but it must also give form and beauty to what is essentially without form and beauty—without form, that is, and consequently without beauty. In short, to present the rock is to falsify it, and to cover it with leaves is to falsify it still more. Stevens knows this, knows that to fix reality even for an instant is to make a fiction. But he knows also, by his seventieth year, that the final belief must be a fiction, and that the wise man realizes that it must be so and chooses consciously and well.

The Collected Poems of Wallace Stevens is such a fiction. The poems oscillate, slowly at first, but then more rapidly, from mind to world and back again until the blur produces a rock, most certain, most sure. Constantly changing, they re-create the process of human experience as they move from sensory perception to thought to imagination to meditation. Taken as a single poem, *The Collected Poems* is a remarkable effort to present a dynamic symbol for a dynamic universe. Taken individually, each poem in the collection is an attempt to present some aspect of experience—experience in its broadest sense, the sense which includes thought and meditation as part of its domain. But always Stevens insists that each poem, and, therefore, every part of experience, is "That which is always beginning because it is part/ Of that which is always beginning, over and over" (CP, p. 530). It is, Stevens knew, impossible to present the "central poem," the "supreme fiction," in any one such aspect of experience, in any single poem. Instead, as he puts it,

> The central poem is the poem of the whole,
> The poem of the composition of the whole,
> The composition of blue sea and of green,
> Of blue light and of green, as lesser poems,
> And the miraculous multiplex of lesser poems,
> Not merely into a whole, but a poem of
> The whole, the essential compact of the parts,
> The roundness that pulls tight the final ring. . . .
>
> (CP, p. 442)

Such a central poem is "The Whole of Harmonium," is *The Collected Poems of Wallace Stevens*. Out of the "miraculous multiplex of lesser poems" emerges a "poem of/ The whole," a sufficient symbol for the truth of human experience in a dynamic world.

Selected Bibliography

Alvarez, A. *Stewards of Excellence*. New York: Charles Scribner's Sons, 1958.

Baker, Howard. "Wallace Stevens," in *The Achievement of Wallace Stevens* . . . , ed. Ashley Brown and Robert S. Haller. Philadelphia: J. B. Lippincott Co., 1962.

Benamou, Michel. "Jules Laforgue and Wallace Stevens," *Romanic Review*, L (1959), 107–17.

———. "Wallace Stevens and the Symbolist Imagination," in *The Act of the Mind: Essays on the Poetry of Wallace Stevens* . . . , ed. Roy Harvey Pearce and J. Hillis Miller. Baltimore: The Johns Hopkins Press, 1965, pp. 92–120.

———. "Wallace Stevens: Some Relations between Poetry and Painting," in *The Achievement of Wallace Stevens* . . . , ed. Ashley Brown and Robert S. Haller. Philadelphia: J. B. Lippincott Co., 1962, pp. 232–48.

Bewley, Marius. "The Poetry of Wallace Stevens," in *The Achievement of Wallace Stevens* . . . , ed. Ashley Brown and Robert S. Haller. Philadelphia: J. B. Lippincott Co., 1962, pp. 141-61.

Blackmur, R. P. "Examples of Wallace Stevens," in *The Achievement of Wallace Stevens* . . . , ed. Ashley Brown and Robert S. Haller. Philadelphia: J. B. Lippincott Co., 1962, pp. 52–81.

———. *Form and Value in Modern Poetry*. Garden City: Anchor Doubleday, 1957.

———. "Substance that Prevails," *Kenyon Review*, XVII (1955), 94–110.

Bloom, Harold. " 'Notes toward a Supreme Fiction': A Commentary," in *Wallace Stevens: A Collection of Critical Essays* . . . , ed. Marie Borroff. Englewood Cliffs: Prentice-Hall, 1963, pp. 76–95.

Borroff, Marie. "Introduction; Wallace Stevens: The World and the Poet," in *Wallace Stevens: A Collection of Critical Essays* . . . , ed. Marie Borroff. Englewood Cliffs: Prentice-Hall, 1963, pp. 1–23.

Breit, Harvey. "Sanity That Is Magic," *Poetry*, LXII (1943), 40–50.

Brown, Merle E. "Concordia Discors in the Poetry of Wallace Stevens," *American Literature*, XXXIV (1962), 246–49.

Buttel, Robert W. "Stevens' 'Two Figures in Dense Violet Night,' " *The Explicator*, IX (1951), item 45.

———. "Wallace Stevens at Harvard: Some Origins of His Theme and Style," in *The Act of the Mind: Essays on the Poetry of Wallace Stevens* . . . , ed. Roy Harvey Pearce and J. Hillis Miller. Baltimore: The Johns Hopkins Press, 1965, pp. 29–57.

———. *Wallace Stevens: The Making of Harmonium.* Princeton: Princeton University Press, 1967.

Cunningham, J. V. "The Poetry of Wallace Stevens," *Poetry*, LXXXV (1949), 149–65.

———. "Tradition and Modernity: Wallace Stevens," in *The Achievement of Wallace Stevens* . . . , ed. Ashley Brown and Robert S. Haller. Philadelphia: J. B. Lippincott Co., 1962, pp. 123–40.

Davie, Donald. " 'The Auroras of Autumn,' " in *The Achievement of Wallace Stevens* . . . , ed. Ashley Brown and Robert S. Haller. Philadelphia: J. B. Lippincott Co., 1962, pp. 166–78.

———. "Essential Gaudiness: The Poems of Wallace Stevens," *Twentieth Century*, CLIII (1953), 455–62.

Doggett, Frank. "The Poet of Earth: Wallace Stevens," *College English*, XXII (1961), 373–80.

———. *Stevens' Poetry of Thought.* Baltimore: The Johns Hopkins Press, 1966.

———. "Stevens' 'Woman Looking at a Vase of Flowers,' " *The Explicator*, XIX (1960), item 7.

———. "This Invented World: Stevens' 'Notes toward a Supreme Fiction,' " in *The Act of the Mind: Essays on the Poetry of Wallace Stevens* . . . , ed. Roy Harvey Pearce and J. Hillis Miller. Baltimore: The Johns Hopkins Press, 1965, pp. 13–28.

———. "Wallace Stevens' Later Poetry," *ELH*, XXV (1958), 137–54.

———. "Wallace Stevens and the World We Know," *English Journal*, XLVIII (1959), 365–73.

Donoghue, Denis. "Nuances of a Theme by Stevens," in *The Act of the Mind: Essays on the Poetry of Wallace Stevens . . . ,* ed. Roy Harvey Pearce and J. Hillis Miller. Baltimore: The Johns Hopkins Press, 1965, pp. 224–42.

Ellman, Richard. "Wallace Stevens' Ice Cream," *Kenyon Review,* XIX (1957), 89–105.

Enck, John J. *Wallace Stevens: Images and Judgements.* Carbondale: Southern Illinois University Press, 1964.

Farnsworth, Robert M. "Stevens' 'So-And-So Reclining on Her Couch,'" *Explicator,* X (1952), item 60.

Ferry, David R. "Stevens' 'Sea Surface Full of Clouds,'" *Explicator,* VI (1948), item 56.

Ford, N. F. "Peter Quince's Orchestra," *MLN,* LXXV (1960), 405–11.

French, Warren. "Stevens' 'The Glass of Water,'" *Explicator,* XIX, iv (January 1961), item 23.

Frye, Northrop. "The Romantic Oriole: A Study of Wallace Stevens," in *Wallace Stevens: A Collection of Critical Essays . . . ,* ed. Marie Borroff. Englewood Cliffs: Prentice-Hall, 1963, 161–76.

Fuchs, Daniel. *The Comic Spirit of Wallace Stevens.* Durham, N.C.: Duke University Press, 1963.

Gay, R. M. "Stevens' 'Le Monocle de Mon Oncle,'" *The Explicator,* VI (1948), item 27.

Guthrie, Ramon. "Stevens' 'Lions in Sweden,'" *Explicator,* XX (1961), item 32.

Hammond, Mac. "On the Grammar of Wallace Stevens," in *The Act of the Mind: Essays on the Poetry of Wallace Stevens . . . ,* ed. Roy Harvey Pearce and J. Hillis Miller. Baltimore: The Johns Hopkins Press, 1965, pp. 179–84.

Hartsack, Mildred E. "Stevens' 'Bantams in Pine-Woods,'" *Explicator,* XVIII (1960), item 1.

Hays, H. R. "Laforgue and Wallace Stevens," *Romanic Review,* XXV (1934), 242–48.

Heringman, Bernard. "Wallace Stevens: One Use of Poetry," in *The Act of the Mind: Essays on the Poetry of Wallace Stevens . . . ,* ed. Roy Harvey Pearce and J. Hillis Miller. Baltimore: The Johns Hopkins Press, 1965, pp. 1–12.

Herzberg, Max, and Wallace Stevens. "Stevens' 'Emperor of Ice Cream,'" *The Explicator*, VII (1948), item 18.

Jarrell, Randall. "*The Collected Poems of Wallace Stevens*," in *The Achievement of Wallace Stevens . . .* , ed. Ashley Brown and Robert S. Haller. Philadelphia: J. B. Lippincott Co., 1962, pp. 179–93.

――――. *Poetry and the Age.* New York: Vantage Press Inc., 1959.

Kermode, Frank. *Wallace Stevens.* London: Oliver and Boyd, 1960.

Lippold, Richard. "Illusion as Structure," in *Modern Culture and the Arts . . .* , ed. James B. Hall and Barry Ulanov. New York: McGraw-Hill, 1967, pp. 214–27.

Logan, L. "John Gruen's Settings for Wallace Stevens," *Hudson Review*, LX (1956), 273–76.

Lowell, Robert. "Imagination and Reality," *The Nation*, CLXVI (1947), 400–402.

Macksey, Richard A. "The Climates of Wallace Stevens," in *The Act of the Mind: Essays on the Poetry of Wallace Stevens . . .* , ed. Roy Harvey Pearce and J. Hillis Miller. Baltimore: The Johns Hopkins Press, 1965, pp. 185–223.

Martz, Louis L. "Wallace Stevens: The World as Meditation," in *Wallace Stevens: A Collection of Critical Essays . . .* , ed. Marie Borroff. Englewood Cliffs: Prentice-Hall, 1963, pp. 211–31.

McFadden, G. "Probings for an Integration: Color Symbolism in Wallace Stevens," *MP*, LVIII (1961), 186–93.

McNamara, Peter L. "The Multi-Faceted Blackbird and Wallace Stevens' Poetic Vision," *College English*, XXV (October–May 1963–64), 446–48.

Miller, J. Hillis. "Wallace Stevens' Poetry of Being," in *The Act of the Mind: Essays on the Poetry of Wallace Stevens . . .* , ed. Roy Harvey Pearce and J. Hillis Miller. Baltimore: The John Hopkins Press, 1965, pp. 143–62.

Mills, Ralph J., Jr. "Wallace Stevens: The Image of the Rock," in *Wallace Stevens: A Collection of Critical Essays . . .* , ed. Marie Borroff. Englewood Cliffs: Prentice-Hall, 1963, pp. 96–110.

Mizner, A. "Not in Cold Blood," *Kenyon Review*, XIII (1951), 218–25.

Monroe, Harriet. "From Mr. Yeats and the Poetic Drama," in *The Achievement of Wallace Stevens . . .* , ed. Ashley Brown and Robert S. Haller. Philadelphia: J. B. Lippincott Co., 1962, pp. 9–21.

Moore, Geoffrey. "Wallace Stevens: A Hero of Our Time," in *The Achievement of Wallace Stevens . . .*, ed. Ashley Brown and Robert S. Haller. Philadelphia: J. B. Lippincott Co., 1962, pp. 249–70.

Moore, Marianne. "Unanimity and Fortitude," *Poetry*, XLIX (1937), 269–72.

——. "Well Moused, Lion," in *The Achievement of Wallace Stevens . . .*, ed. Ashley Brown and Robert S. Haller. Philadelphia: J. B. Lippincott Co., 1962, pp. 21–29.

——. "The World Imagined . . . Since We Are Poor," in *The Achievement of Wallace Stevens . . .*, ed. Ashley Brown and Robert S. Haller. Philadelphia: J. B. Lippincott Co., 1962, pp. 162–65.

Moorman, Charles. "Stevens' 'Six Significant Landscapes,'" *Explicator*, XVII (1958), item 1.

Morse, Samuel French. "Introduction," *Opus Posthumous*, New York: Alfred A. Knopf, 1959.

——. "Introduction," *Selected Poems by Wallace Stevens*. New York: Vintage Books, 1959.

——. "The Native Element," in *The Achievement of Wallace Stevens . . .*, ed. Ashley Brown and Robert S. Haller. Philadelphia: J. B. Lippincott Co., 1962, pp. 193–210.

——. "Wallace Stevens, Bergson, Pater," in *The Act of the Mind: Essays on the Poetry of Wallace Stevens . . .*, ed. Roy Harvey Pearce and J. Hillis Miller. Baltimore: The Johns Hopkins Press, 1965, pp. 48–92.

Munson, Gorham. "The Dandyism of Wallace Stevens," in *The Achievement of Wallace Stevens . . .*, ed. Ashley Brown and Robert S. Haller. Philadelphia: J. B. Lippincott Co., 1962, pp. 41–45.

Nassar, Eugene Paul. *Wallace Stevens: An Anatomy of Figuration*. Philadelphia: University of Pennsylvania Press, 1965.

Nemerov, Howard. "The Poetry of Wallace Stevens," *Sewanee Review*, LXV (1957), 1–14.

O'Connor, William Van. *The Shaping Spirit: A Study of Wallace Stevens*. Chicago: Henry Regnery, 1950.

Olson, Elder. "The Poetry of Wallace Stevens," *College English*, XVI (1955), 395–402.

Pack, Robert. *Wallace Stevens: An Approach to His Poetry and Thought*. New Brunswick, N.J.: Rutgers University Press, 1958.

Pearce, Roy Harvey. "Wallace Stevens: The Last Lesson of the Master," in *The Act of the Mind: Essays on the Poetry of*

Wallace Stevens. Baltimore: The Johns Hopkins Press, 1965, pp. 121–42.

———. "Wallace Stevens: The Life of the Imagination," in *Wallace Stevens: A Collection of Critical Essays . . .*, ed. Marie Borroff. Englewood Cliffs: Prentice-Hall, 1963, pp. 111–32.

Peckham, Morse. "Toward a Theory of Romanticism," *PMLA,* LXVI, ii (March 1951), 5–23.

Powys, Llewelyn. "The Thirteenth Way," in *The Achievement of Wallace Stevens . . .* , ed. Ashley Brown and Robert S. Haller. Philadelphia: J. B. Lippincott Co., 1962, pp. 29–34.

Quinn, Sister M. Bernetta. "Metamorphosis in Wallace Stevens," in *Wallace Stevens: A Collection of Critical Essays . . .* , ed. Marie Borroff. Englewood Cliffs: Prentice-Hall, 1963, pp. 54–71.

Ransom, John Crowe. "Artists, Soldiers, Positivists," *Kenyon Review,* VI (Spring 1944), 276–77.

Riddel, Joseph N. "Authorship of Wallace Stevens' 'On Poetic Truth,' " *MLN,* LXXVI (1961), 126–29.

———. *The Clairvoyant Eye: The Poetry and Poetics of Wallace Stevens.* Baton Rouge: Louisiana State University Press, 1965.

———. "The Contours of Stevens' Criticism," in *The Act of the Mind: Essays on the Poetry of Wallace Stevens . . .* , ed. Roy Harvey Pearce and J. Hillis Miller. Baltimore: The Johns Hopkins Press, 1965, pp. 243–76.

———. "Disguised Pronunciamento: Wallace Stevens' 'Sea Surfaces,' " *Texas Studies in English,* XXXVII (1958), 177–86.

———. "Wallace Stevens' 'Visibility of Thought,' " *PMLA,* LXXVII, iv (September 1962), 482–98.

———. "Walt Whitman and Wallace Stevens: Functions of a Literatus," in *Wallace Stevens: A Collection of Critical Essays . . .* , ed. Marie Borroff. Englewood Cliffs: Prentice-Hall, 1963, pp. 30–42.

Rosenthal, M. L. *The Modern Poets.* New York: Oxford University Press, 1960.

———. "Stevens' 'Sea Surface Full of Clouds,' " *The Explicator,* XIX (1961), item 38.

Rosenfeld, Paul. "Wallace Stevens," in *The Achievement of Wallace Stevens . . .* , ed. Ashley Brown and Robert S. Haller. Philadelphia: J. B. Lippincott Co., 1962, pp. 35–40.

Schwartz, Delmore. "Instructed of Much Mortality," *Sewanee Review,* LIX (1946), 439–49.

Silverstein, Norman. "Stevens' 'Of Hartford in a Purple Light,' " *The Explicator*, XVIII (1959), item 20.

Simons, Hi. " 'The Comedian as the Letter C': Its Sense and Significance," in *The Achievement of Wallace Stevens . . . ,* ed. Ashley Brown and Robert S. Haller. Philadelphia: J. B. Lippincott Co., 1962, pp. 97–114.

––––––. "The Genre of Wallace Stevens," in *Wallace Stevens: A Collection of Critical Essays . . . ,* ed. Marie Borroff. Englewood Cliffs: Prentice-Hall, 1963, pp. 43–53.

––––––. "The Humanism of Wallace Stevens," *Poetry*, LXI (1942), 448–52.

––––––. "Wallace Stevens and Mallarmé," *MP*, XLIII (1946), 235–59.

Smith, Hugh L. "Stevens' 'Life Is Motion,' " *Explicator*, XIX, vii (April 1961), item 48.

Stallknecht, N. P. "Absence in Reality: A Study in the Epistemology of the Blue Guitar," *Kenyon Review*, XXI (1959), 545–62.

Stevens, Wallace. *The Collected Poems of Wallace Stevens*. New York: Alfred A. Knopf, 1957.

––––––. *Letters of Wallace Stevens . . . ,* ed. and selected by Holly Stevens. New York: Alfred A. Knopf, 1966.

––––––. *The Necessary Angel*. New York: Alfred A. Knopf, 1951.

––––––. *Opus Posthumous . . . ,* ed. and with an introduction by Samuel French Morse. New York: Alfred A. Knopf, 1957.

Stocking, Fred H. "Stevens' 'Peter Quince at the Clavier,' " *Explicator*, V, vii (May 1947), item 47.

Storm, Mary Joan. "Stevens' 'Peter Quince at the Clavier,' " *Explicator*, XIV (1955), item 9.

Symons, Julian. "A Short View of Wallace Stevens," in *The Achievement of Wallace Stevens . . . ,* ed. Ashley Brown and Robert S. Haller. Philadelphia: J. B. Lippincott Co., 1962, pp. 114–22.

Therese, Sister, S. N. D. "Stevens' 'The Glass of Water,' " *Explicator*, XXI, vii (March 1963), item 56.

Tindall, William York. *Wallace Stevens*. Minneapolis: University of Minnesota Press, 1961.

Vendler, Helen Hennessy. "The Qualified Assertions of Wallace Stevens," in *The Act of the Mind: Essays on the Poetry of Wallace Stevens . . . ,* ed. Roy Harvey Pearce and J. Hillis Miller. Baltimore: The Johns Hopkins Press, 1965, pp. 163–78.

Wagner, C. Roland. "A Central Poetry," in *Wallace Stevens: A Collection of Critical Essays . . .* , ed. Marie Borroff. Englewood Cliffs: Prentice-Hall, 1963, pp. 71–75.

Walsh, Thomas. *A Concordance to the Poetry of Wallace Stevens.* University Park, Pa.: Pennsylvania State University Press, 1963.

Wells, Henry W. *Introduction to Wallace Stevens.* Bloomington: Indiana University Press, 1964.

Winters, Yvor. *In Defense of Reason.* New York: Swallow Press and William Morrow, 1947.

Zabel, Morton D. "The Harmonium of Wallace Stevens," in *The Achievement of Wallace Stevens . . .* , ed. Ashley Brown and Robert S. Haller. Philadelphia: J. B. Lippincott Co., 1962, pp. 46–52.

————. "Wallace Stevens and the Image of Man," in *Wallace Stevens: A Collection of Critical Essays . . .* , ed. Marie Borroff. Englewood Cliffs: Prentice-Hall, 1963, pp. 151–60.

Index

Stevens, Wallace: 1; use of organic metaphor, 2; reputation and critical appraisal; 1–2; idea of "grand poem," 3; modernity of, 6; ability to appeal to the senses, 9; images for reality and the imagination, 105, 151

"Study of Two Pears," 67–68

Summer. *See* Imagination, figures of

Sun. *See* "Reality," figures of

"Sunday Morning," 9, 22, 41, 53, 63, 108–14 *passim*

"Sun this March, The," 38

Supreme Fiction: Stevens' comments upon, 114–17; mentioned, 56, 78, 84, 90, 91, 97, 109, 116, 139, 140, 141, 164, 172

"Tea at the Palaz of Hoon," 15

"Thinking of a Relation between the Images of Metaphors," 95–97

"Thirteen Ways of Looking at a Blackbird," 23, 25–31, 70

Thoreau, Henry David, 72–73

"Thought Revolved, A," 60–63, 70

"Three Academic Pieces," 97

"To an Old Philosopher in Rome," 153–54

Transformation, images of: in "Comedian as the Letter C," 20–21; awakening, 71–75 *passim;* in *Auroras of Autumn* and *Ideas of Order,* 119; in "Auroras of Autumn," 134; in *The Rock,* 162–63

Trinity College, 93

Ulysses, 156–57

Uruguay, Mrs. Alfred, 169

"Vacancy in the Park," 157–58

Walden, 73

War, 80, 82, 87, 112

"Weak Mind in the Mountains, A," 73

"What We See Is What We Think," 125–26, 163

Whitehead, Alfred North, 100

"Whole of Harmonium": Stevens' use of term, ix, 3; as organic symbol, 4–5, 172; significance to Stevens' stature as poet, 6; exclusion of *Owl's Clover* from, 51–52

"Woman in Sunshine, The," 123

Wordsworth, William, 6, 31

"World as Meditation, The," 155–57, 159

Yeats, William Butler, 31